KV-576-533

Gran Canaria
and the Eastern
Canary Islands

A Travel Guide

Mary and Archie Tisdall

Roger Lascelles, Cartographic and Travel Publisher
47 York Road, Brentford, Middlesex TW8 0QP Telephone: 01-847 0935

Publication Data

Title	Gran Canaria and the Eastern Canary Islands
Typeface	Phototypeset in Compugraphic English 18
Photographs	By the Authors.
Printing	Kelso Graphics, Kelso, Scotland
ISBN	0 903909 27 8
Edition	This first June, 1984
Publisher	Roger Lascelles 47 York Road, Brentford, Middlesex, TW8 0QP.
Copyright	Mary & Archie Tisdall

Distribution

Africa: Enquiries invited

Americas: Canada — International travel maps & books,
P.O. Box 2290, Vancouver B.C.

U.S.A. — Bradt Enterprises, 95 Harvey Street.,
Cambridge, MA. 02140 U.S.A.

Asia: Hong Kong — The Book Society, G.P.Q. Box 7804
Hong Kong Tel: 5-241901
India — English Book Store, New Delhi

Australasia Australia — Rex Map Centre, 413 Pacific Highway,
Artarmon NSW 2064
New Zealand — International Travel Guides, P.O.
Box 4397, Christchurch 1

Europe: Belgium — Brussels, Peuples et Continents
GB/Ireland — Available through all booksellers with
a good foreign travel section.
Italy — Libreria dell'Automobile, Milano
Netherlands — Nilsson & Lamm BV, Weesp
Denmark — Copenhagen — Arnold Busck,
G.E.C. Gad, Boghallen
Finland — Oslo - Arne Gimnes J.G. Tanum
Sweden — Stockholm - Esselte/Akademi Bokhandel
Fritzes/Hedengrens
Gothenburg - Gumperts/Esselte
Lund - Gleerupska
Switzerland — The Travel Bookshop,
Seilergraben 11, 8001 Zurich
Librairie Artou, 8 rue de Rive, 1204
Geneve.

Mary and Archie Tisdall have had a life of travel which many would envy. Archie served in the Royal Air Force for 40 years and during this time they lived in such diverse countries as Singapore, Jordan, Libya, Tunisia and Malta.

Towards retirement they bought a motor caravan to enable them to visit further places abroad, principally in western Europe and gradually they began to write of their experiences.

They have enjoyed no less than five winters in the Canary Islands and have built up a reservoir of knowledge which manifests itself in this book and its sister title.

They have two sons and two daughters, and when not travelling they live in Salisbury, Wiltshire.

Foreword

'Across the Seas we beheld Seven Islands,
each with its own special delight'

This guide has been written with the object of enlightening the reader as to the many delights of the golden Canary Islands. The Canaries consist of seven main islands which lie in the Atlantic, some seventy miles (112 km) west of North Africa. They are divided into Western and Eastern Provinces.

With a wonderful climate all the year, sandy beaches, duty free shopping, entertainments and exotic landscapes — they are a paradise for the holiday maker.

Details are given explaining how to get there, costs, where and when to travel, with plenty of information about accommodation, attractions and local life. Facts and information are as accurate as possible at the time of going to press. The exchange rate quoted, 194 pesetas to £1, was average at the time the book was written (1983). Being duty free islands, you get good value for your money as many items are tax free.

This guide describes the Eastern Islands: Gran Canaria, Lanzarote and Fuerteventura.

Its sister volume describes the Western Islands: Tenerife, La Palma, Gomera and El Hierro.

Most of all we hope that these books will help you to know, visit and enjoy the Canary Islands, as we have done.

Font Cover: One of the many sandy beaches in the Eastern Canary Islands, this one is on the north coast of Fuerteventura looking north east to the island of Los Lobos with Lanzarote in the distance.

Contents

1. Why the Canary Islands?

The charm of the Canaries

One of the delights of the Canary Islands is the knowledge that you will be able to enjoy a climate that is warm and sunny, yet remains fresh and spring-like all the year.

Seven large islands and six small islets form the Canary archipelago in the Atlantic Ocean, 112 km west of North Africa on a line with the Bahamas and 480 km north of the Tropics. These are happy peaceful islands, whose people welcome visitors with a natural friendliness.

The Canary Islands are easily accessible by air and sea, and there is accommodation to suit every taste and pocket, from top class hotel, modern apartment, pretty villa to simple guest-house. Constant sun shines from clear blue skies over land-scapes that are so diverse that the islands have been described as a 'continent in miniature'. There is a wonderful choice of pastimes and pleasures. Sunbathing, swimming and a variety of sports can be enjoyed daily. The main tourist resorts offer a wide range of entertainments, including a lively night life, with plenty of bars and restaurants, music and dancing.

The Canaries are where you can enjoy breakfast on a sunlit terrace, take a drive into the mountains amid green forests of sweetly perfumed pine and heather, walk amongst sand dunes or ride a camel. Lunch at a little fishing village while watching fishermen mending their nets; where you can laze the after-noon away on a golden beach, then go shopping in an Arab Souk or visit a needlework school. In the evening you can stroll along the *plazas* with the Canarians, and have a cool drink on a colour-ful patio while the sun goes down over calm waters; dine by moonlight at a table under the stars, watch folk dancing, and go on to a disco or night club.

The Canary Islands have so much to offer the visitor; with their vast mountains, dense forests, green valleys, black volcanic landscapes and golden beaches, they must surely be the most delightful of all holiday destinations.

Welcome to the Canary Islands.

Visitors to the Canaries — 1982

Tenerife Province
Number of European Tourists	1,459,459
Number of British Tourists	412,372

Las Palmas Province
Number of European Tourists	1,200,938
Number of British Tourists	112,153

Combined total of British Tourists	524,525

Their situation

The Canary Islands are an archipelago of seven major islands, Tenerife, Gomera, La Palma, El Hierro, Gran Canaria, Lanzarote and Fuerteventura, and six small islets, Isla de los Lobos, Isla Graciosa, Isla de Montana Clara, Isla de Alegranza, Roque del Oeste and Roque del Este. The islands are situated in the Atlantic Ocean 112 kms west of Morocco and 1120 kms south of Spain, at a latitude of 28°. They are south of the islands of Madeira. The area of the archipelago is in the region of 7500 sq. km. The Tropic of Cancer lies 480 km to the south.

The appearance of the Canary Islands indicates that they were formed by a number of violent volcanic eruptions many years ago so there is much evidence of volcanic cones and lava. The highest point of eruption was Mount Teide, in Tenerife.

Generally speaking the five most westerly islands, Gran Canaria, Tenerife, La Palma, Gomera and El Hierro are more mountainous and green. Lanzarote and Fuerteventura being dry desert are immensely interesting and similar to parts of North Africa. The islands tend to have steep coastal cliffs in the north while the southern coasts are more level. Except for Lanzarote all have central high mountains.

The islands' features are rocky mountains, thick forests, deeply wooded ravines, fertile plains, volcanic wasteland and stretches of sand dunes. The best beaches are mainly on the east and south coasts. Some are pure golden or white, others are volcanic black sand.

Five small islets lie off the north of Lanzarote, called Graciosa, Alegranza, Montana Clara, Roque del Oeste and Roque del Este.

The islet of Graciosa is 42 sq kms in area and can be clearly seen from Lanzarote, just a kilometre away. The population of 800 reside mainly at Caleta del Sebo, living by fishing and visits from tourists. Lovely golden beaches have been earmarked for future development. The other four islets are uninhabited, except for sea birds.

Between Lanzarote and Fuerteventura is the islet of Los Lobos, just 6.5 sq kms. The only village is El Puertito, where the fishermen supplement their income from the holidaymakers who visit from Corralejo, the port in the north of Fuerteventura. Day trips can be made only when the sea is calm. The channel between Fuerteventura and Los Lobos, called La Bocaina, is noted for its strong currents and huge Atlantic rollers. It is also a plentiful fishing ground.

Climate

The Canary Islands are warm and fresh with spring-like weather. The mean temperature varies between 25°C and 18°C, with many days of brilliant sunshine; midday temperatures can reach 32°C, or more. The average sea temperature in winter is 18°C and in summer 22°C, making all year round swimming possible.

The small amount of rain falls mainly in the north of the islands, where it is more green with a humidity of between 60% and 69%. The rainfall is governed by the mountains on each island and varies accordingly. Tenerife and Gran Canaria have more rainfall than Lanzarote and Fuerteventura. Rain is heaviest between November and February — June, July and August being the driest months.

Winds are predominantly northwesterly (*Los Alisos*) occasionally veering to easterly when they bring hot air and dusty sand from North Africa. The latter wind is called *sirocco* and usually lasts three to four days. Because of the light breezes that blow most days, the climate is invigorating and gives a sense of well being.

And because of the mountains and the fact that the islands are small land masses, there can be considerable change in the weather on the same day. The north can be cloudy while the south remains sunny. There is a saying that somewhere on every island there is sunshine every day.

The sun sinks quickly in these latitudes giving short evenings so often spectacular sunsets are seen. The nights can be very clear and conducive to star gazing. Because of the clear air an Astro-Physical Observatory has recently been built on the island of La Palma.

Sufferers from bronchitis, influenza and asthma find much relief when staying in the Canary Islands, especially during the winter months. However those suffering from respiratory ailments should not settle in the city of Las Palmas, Gran Canaria, because of the acknowledged pollution problem caused by traffic congestion, dust from building projects and the occasional *sirocco* dust storm from the Sahara Desert.

Thus, one of the biggest incentives to visit the Canary Islands is its predictable climate. With so little variation during the year and from one year to another, visitors can be assured of sunshine practically every day. Even if there is cloud, it will not be cold. The few rainy days do not last for long, then the sun shines again.

Playa de las Canteras, Las Palmas, claimed as one of the World's top ten, international beaches. Over two kilometres long with golden sands and warm water.

Climatic Chart

Average temp.

	Jan	Feb	Mar	Apr	May	Jun	Jul	Aug	Sep	Oct	Nov	Dec	Yearly
C	17.8	17.9	18.5	19.3	20.4	22.0	23.6	24.2	24.0	23.5	21.5	18.8	21.7
F	64.0	64.2	65.3	66.7	68.7	71.6	74.4	75.5	75.2	74.3	70.7	65.8	71
Humidity %	67	67	66	64	63	63	59	60	65	68	69	67.0	65
Cloudy days	2	1	0	0	1	0	0	0	0	0	1	2.0	7
Clear days	6	6	6	8	7	8	11	12	9	6	3	4.0	86
Sunny days	18	16	20	18	18	16	13	12	17	18	17	16.0	199
Rainy days	7.5	6	4 9	4	2	1	1	1	2	6	10	9.0	54

When to go

The Canary Islands are ideal for all-the-year-round holidays. During the summer months a high proportion of Spanish nationals visit the islands. During the period October to May, the majority of visitors come from the cooler climates of Germany, Scandinavia, Holland and France. Many local shop keepers and restaurant owners take their holidays during the month of June, which (they say) can be a slack month. It is also the cheapest travel period for package tours. The peak period is from November to February when a high percentage of the accommodation is booked in advance; this is the time of the year when most tourists from the UK arrive. Christmas and New Year is the most expensive period but good value.

Because of the constant demand in the most popular tourist areas of Puerto de la Cruz in Tenerife, Playa del Inglés in Gran Canaria and Puerto del Carmen in Lanzarote, it is advisable to plan ones visit well in advance, especially over the Christmas period.

Some hotels and apartments have tariff variation as follows:

Low season — 1 May to 30 June
Mid season — 1 July to 31 October
High season — 1 November to 30 April

Tourist information

Visitors to the Canary Islands require a valid passport, which must be stamped by the Spanish Immigration Authority on entry, with arrival date. It is your responsibility to see this done, otherwise your entry is illegal. You do not need a visa for a stay of up to 90 days, but after this it may be necessary. Information can be obtained from: The Spanish Consulate, 20 Draycott Place, London SW3. Tel: 01 581 5921.

Up to date tourist information can be obtained from: The Spanish National Tourist Office, 57/58 St. James's Street, London SW1. Tel: 01 499 0901.

Vaccinations are not normally needed for the Canary Islands. Only in the case of an epidemic would they be required.

Visitors are allowed to bring in any amount of foreign currency in notes or travellers cheques and up to 150,000 pesetas. You may take out 20,000 pesetas and foreign currency equivalent to 80,000 pesetas (£412).

Spanish Tourist Offices

The Spanish Tourist Industry is organised through the Secretaria de Estado, part of the Ministerio de Transportes, Turismo and Comunicaciones and funded by the State. The Secretaria has a delegation in the capital of each province and public information offices are also there.

Oficinas Municipales de Turismo are situated in towns and villages of particular tourist interest and are there to provide information, free of charge. It is recommended that use be made of these tourist offices in the Canary Islands; they can supply lists of accommodation, island and town maps, literature often with good pictures. Although in some offices the staff may only have a limited knowledge of English, much effort is made to assist tourists. They can be found in:

Western Province

Tenerife —	Palacio Insular, Santa Cruz de Tenerife. Tel: 24 22 27.
La Palma —	Calle O'Daly, Santa Cruz de la Palma.
Gomera —	Ayuntamiento, General Franco 20, San Sebastián.
El Hierro —	Cabildo Insular del Hierro, Valverde.

Eastern Province

Gran Canaria —	Parque Santa Catalina, Las Palmas. Tel: 26 46 23.
Lanzarote —	Parque Municipale, Arrecife.
Fuerteventura —	Ministero de Trabajo, Avenida General Franco, Puerto del Rosario.

Arrival by air

Of the seven islands, La Gomera is the only one that does not have an airport but there is a project to build one near Santiago in the south of the island. (However there are frequent ferries from Santa Cruz de Tenerife and Los Cristianos in the south of Tenerife to San Sebastián de la Gomera.

The Airports of the Canaries

Tenerife	— Aeropuerto Los Rodeos (Inter Island)
	— Aeropuerto Reina Sofia (International)
Gran Canaria	— Aeropuerto de Gando
Fuerteventura	— Aeropuerto Los Estancas (Puerto del Rosario)
Lanzarote	— Aeropuerto de Lanzarote (Arrecife)
El Hierro	— Aeropuerto del Hierro (Valverde)
La Palma	— Aeropuerto de la Palma

The airport at El Hierro is virtually a landing strip, but it is of good size and sufficient for the two return flights each day between Tenerife and El Hierro.

On all the other islands the airports are modern and efficient and well able to cope with the traffic, which sometimes is very heavy.

The system for handling passengers and their luggage is the same as for all international airports and the Spanish have no wish to slow the flow of tourists. It is necessary only to have your passport stamped with the date of entry. The airports are well served with taxis and buses. Booking arrangements for hotels, apartments and car rental at Tenerife, Gran Canaria and Lanzarote can be made from the airport.

The airport at Lanzarote deserves a special mention, being designed by the local born César Manrique. The interior decor is green and white, the ceiling is lined with green and white canvas. There is green upholstered seating and many potted palms and ferns. It resembles the lounge of a luxury hotel or a tent belonging to a rich sultan!

Further airport information is given in the chapters dealing with individual islands.

Air services

The only scheduled air service direct to the Canaries is provided by the Spanish state airline: **Iberia,** 169 Regent Street, London W1RBE. Tel: 01 437 5622.

There are scheduled flights from London, via Madrid, to the Canary Islands. The return fare being about £200.

There are several charter flights used by package operators, which fly direct between the UK and the Canary Islands. Seats on these aircraft are sometimes available, without accommodation. Travel Agents are able to supply details. Prices vary according to the season but can be lower than those of Iberia.

The flight time between London/Gatwick and Gran Canaria/Las Palmas is 4 hours and to Lanzarote/Arrecife is 3¾ hours.

There are no direct flights to Fuerteventura but there are inter-island air services from Tenerife.

Inter Island Flight Times

Gando Airport ·	to	Reina Sophia/Los Rodeos		
Las Palmas		(Tenerife)	—	35 mins
(Gran Canaria)	to	Los Estancos		
		(Fuerteventura)	—	30 mins
	to	La Palma		
		(La Palma)	—	40 mins
	to	Arrecife		
		(Lanzarote)	—	35 mins

Arrival by sea (from Cadiz)

The only car and passenger ferry service operating from Spain to the Canary Islands is from Cadiz (southern Spain) to Tenerife and Gran Canaria, and it is operated by the Trasmediterranea (Aucona) S.A. Shipping Company. It is not possible to go directly to the other islands, though there are ferries to La Palma, El Hierro and Gomera from Tenerife, and to Lanzarote and Fuerteventura from Gran Canaria. But first you have to get to Cadiz ...

By rail to Cadiz

Rail tickets for travel from UK to Cadiz, Spain, can be obtained from:

British Rail Continental Ltd., Ticket and Information Office, PO Box No. 29, London SW1V1JX. Tel: 01 834 2345

or through a Travel Agent. There are no Spanish Railway Agents in UK. Example of rail fare: Senior Citizen, inclusive travel, London to Cadiz, First Class Return — £90; Second Class Return — £73.60.

Ordinary, inclusive travel, London to Cadiz, Second Class Return — £151.80.

By road to Cadiz

The most direct way is to cross from Plymouth (Devon) to Santander in northern Spain and then drive south to Cadiz (see section Driving in Spain — p. 49).

Brittany Ferries operate a regular car and passenger ferry (from Millbay Docks, Plymouth) throughout the year. The crossing takes twenty-four hours in fully stabilized ships. Driving into the car deck is a simple operation. The ships are comfortable with air-conditioned de luxe, two- and four-berth cabins, some with showers and toilets. There are wide promenade and sun decks, lounges with bars and dance floor, restaurant, duty free shop, cinema, games and children's room.

Arriving in Santander, there are many routes across Spain, the most direct being via Burgos, Madrid, Cordoba and Sevilla to Cadiz. Distance on this route is 1165 km.

One can cross to France by using any of the Channel ports and travel overland to Spain, thence down to Cadiz in the south. However, during the winter months the mountain passes in northern Spain and Andorra can be closed by snow. An alternative route is to drive down to the French Mediterranean and continue along the east coast line of Spain to reach Cadiz.

Yet another variation is to reach Spain and drive along the north coast, then down the western coast into Portugal and along the Algarve to Spain and Cadiz. The latter route, though much longer, gives a very scenic drive.

Examples of ferry costs (these vary with type of accommodation and length of vehicle):

Brittany Ferries

	High	Low Season
Plymouth to Santander		
Car and 2 persons, tourist single	£307	£221
Portsmouth to St Malo		·
Plymouth to Roscoff		
Car and two persons, tourist single	£164	£98

Townsend Thoresen

	High	Low Season
Portsmouth to Le Havre		
Portsmouth to Cherbourg		
Southampton to Le Havre		
Car and two persons, single	£100	£48

Brittany Ferries, Millbay Docks, Plymouth PO7 8RU. Tel: 0752 21321.

The Brittany Centre, Wharf Road, Portsmouth, PO7 8RU. Tel: 0705 827701.

Townsend Thoresen, Russell Street, Dover, CT16 1QB. Tel: 0304 204040.

P. & O. Ferries, Freepost, Southampton, SO91BG.

Sealink Travel Ltd., PO Box 29, Victoria Station, London, SW1V 1JX. Tel: 01 834 8122.

The small ferry ship of the Alisur Company, which sails daily between Playa Blanca, Lanzarote and Corralejo, Fuerteventura. A crossing that takes half an hour.

Tourists enjoy the winter sunshine at Playa Maspalomas, where restaurants and bars serve meals and drinks on the tiled promenade. A few minutes walk leads to the sand dunes and beach.

The Ferry from Cadiz (Trasmediterranea Shipping Co.)

During the winter months there is one ferry a week sailing between Cadiz (in southern Spain) and the Canary Islands. During the summer (2 June to 6 October) it crosses every two days. The ferry calls at Santa Cruz de Tenerife and Las Palmas de Gran Canaria on every voyage, taking nearly two days to get there. This is the only ferry service operating between the Spanish peninsula and the Canaries. It is advisable to book well in advance.

There are two ferry ships operating the service at present, the 'J.J. Sister' and the 'Manuel Soto'. They are similar, of about 10,000 tons each carrying 743 passengers and 250 vehicles. Described as floating hotels, they have a swimming pool, a la carte restaurant, self-service cafeteria, bars, sport facilities, reading room, dance floor, cinema, television, shop, hairdresser, children's playroom and lifts. First and Tourist Class, two, three and four berth cabin accommodation.

The Trasmediterranea ferry ships operating between the islands are smaller but services are adequate considering that the voyages are of shorter duration, about seven hours and usually travel overnight. First and Tourist Class accommodation is provided. All Trasmediterranea ferries have vehicle space, which is drive-on/drive-off. On occasions it may be necessary to reverse on to the car deck.

Trasmediterranea also provide a Jetfoil service between Las Palmas de Gran Canaria and Santa Cruz de Tenerife. It is very fast, taking only eighty minutes, and there are four services a day. Popular with business people and day trippers. Foot passengers only, the single fare is 2850 pesetas (£14.50).

UK Agents for Transmediterranea are:

Townsend Thoresen, 1 Camden Crescent, Dover, Kent. Tel: 0304 202822.

In Europe (UK Office):

Melia Travel Agencies, 12 Dover Street, London W1. Tel: 01 499 6731.

Reservations can also be made in Spain through travel agents. Trasmediterranea have offices in a number of towns in Spain.

In Cadiz: Avenida de Carranza, 26. Tel: 28 43 50. Telex 76028.
In Madrid: (Head Office) Plaza Manuel Gomez Moreno. Tel: 456 00 07. Telex 27731.
In Las Palmas: Aucona, Muelle Santa Catalina. Tel: 26 00 70.
In Santa Cruz de Tenerife: Aucona, Marina 59. Tel: 28 78 50.

The southern corner of Gran Canaria has an extra share of sunshine. Puerto Rico with its sandy beach, is very popular with all tourists and the two harbours have good moorings for many different small craft.

Puerto Rico, always reliable for sunshine, attracts many day tourists from other parts of Gran Canaria with its safe swimming and water sports.

The Inter Island Ferry Services

Trasmediterranea Shipping Company

Las Palmas de Gran Canaria to Arrecife, Lanzarote, calling at Puerto del Rosario, Fuerteventura:

Departs Tuesday, Thursdays and Sundays at 2300 hrs.

Arrives Puerto del Rosario at 0600 hrs. following morning and Arrecife at 1000 hrs.

Las Palmas de Gran Canaria to Santa Cruz de Tenerife:

Departs Mondays and Fridays at 0900 and 1900 hrs.

Tuesdays and Saturdays at 1000 and 1800 hrs, Wednesdays at 1400 hrs, Thursdays at 100 hrs, Sundays at 1900 hrs.

Crossing time 3½ hours.

Jetfoil Service from Las Palmas de Gran Canaria to Santa Cruz de Tenerife:

Departs daily at 0730, 0930 (except Sunday), 1500 and 1700 hrs.

Crossing time 80 minutes.

The inter islands Trasmediterranea ferry services are usually pleasant sea crossings, allowing sunbathing during the day and a cabin or couchette for night journeys. A bar and cafeteria service is available.

Alisur Car and Passenger Ferry

The Alisur Ferry Company provides a daily service between Corralejo in the north of Fuerteventura and Playa Blanca, south Lanzarote taking about 45 minutes. It is a small passenger and car (drive on/drive off) ferry. It is cheaper than the Trasmediterranea Ferry between Puerto del Rosario and Arrecife.

Departure times 6daily)

Playa Blanca (Lanzarote)	—	0720	0930	1630 hrs
Corralejo (Feurteventura)	—	0820	1030	1730 hrs

Fares

Passenger, single	—	1250 pesetas (£6.50)
Vehicle and two passengers, return	—	5,000 pesetas (£25)

Cruises

The following companies operate inclusive luxury liner cruises to the Canary Islands:

Fred Olsen Line, 11 Conduit Street, London. Tel: 01 409 2019.

P & O 'Princess' and 'Canberra' Cruises, Beaufort House, St. Botolph Street, London EC3. Tel: 01 377 2551.

Costa Cruises, Costa Line, 16 Maddox Street, London.

CTC Lines, 1 Lower Regent Street, London W1. Tel: 01 930 5833

Cunard, 8 Berkeley Street, London. Tel: 01 491 3930.

Island Cruises

The Trasmediterranea Shipping and Ferry Company provide pleasure cruises between the islands. The three- and four-day cruises include cabin, meals and entertainment on board, also excursions around the islands visited. These are available all the year round, are popular and of good value.

Cruise ships call at Santa Cruz de Tenerife, Las Palmas de la Gran Canaria, Arrecife (Lanzarote) and Puerto del Rosario (Fuerteventura).

Example Las Palmas (Gran Canaria), Lanzarote, Tenerife and La Palma, Tenerife, Las Palmas — about 19,100 pesetas (£98).

2300 hrs — Saturday	—	Embark Las Palmas
0800 hrs — Sunday	—	Arrive Lanzarote
0930 hrs — Sunday	—	Coach tour of Lanzarote
2000 hrs — Sunday	—	Return to ship
2100 hrs — Sunday	—	Dinner and entertainment
1230 hrs — Monday	—	Arrive Tenerife, tour of island
2100 hrs — Monday	—	Return to ship
2200 hrs — Monday	—	Dinner and dancing
0700 hrs — Tuesday	—	Arrive Santa Cruz de la Palma
0930 hrs — Tuesday	—	Coach tour of La Palma
2000 hrs — Tuesday	—	Return to ship
2100 hrs — Tuesday	—	Dinner, entertainment and dancing
0700 hrs — Wednesday	—	Arrive Santa Cruz de Tenerife
0900 hrs — Wednesday	—	Depart Santa Cruz de Tenerife
1200 hrs — Wednesday	—	Arrive Las Palmas and disembark

Ports in the Canaries

The location of the ports on each island where ferries, car ferries, jetfoil and cruise liners arrive and depart are:

Tenerife
Santa Cruz: All services.
Los Cristianos: Trasmediterranea to Gomera; Alisur to Gomera; Gomera Ferry (to Gomera).

La Palma
Santa Cruz: Trasmediterranea to Santa Cruz de Tenerife.

Gomera
San Sebastián: Transmediterranea to Santa Cruz de Tenerife and Los Cristianos; Alisur Ferry to Los Cristianos, Tenerife; Gomera Ferry to Los Cristianos, Tenerife.

El Hierro
Puerto de la Estaca: Trasmediterranea to Santa Cruz de Tenerife and Gomera.

Trasmediterranea Ferry 'J.J. Sister' one of the two which operate between Cadiz and the Canary Islands.

Gran Canaria
Las Palmas: All services.
Lanzarote
Arrecife: Trasmediterranea to Las Palmas, Gran Canaria.
Playa Blanca: Alisur Ferry to Corralejo, Fuerteventura.
Fuerteventura
Puerto del Rosario: Trasmediterranea to Las Palmas, Gran Canaria; Arrecife, Lanzarote.
Corralejo: Alisur Ferry to Playa Blanca, Lanzarote.

Arrival by Yacht

For those who have the necessary skills and a suitable yacht, it is possible to reach the Canary Islands, though it is well to realise they are in the Atlantic Ocean, not the Mediterranean. For up to date details write to:
National Assembly of Yacht Captains, Muelle Espana, Zona Deportiva, Barcelona, Spain; or
The Spanish Sailing Federation, Juan Vigon 23, Madrid, Spain.

Yacht and Boat facilities

The Canary Islands are ideally situated for yachts and motor vessels, having many suitable marinas and moorings, natural sheltered bays and harbours. Many boats moor there for the winter season, some waiting, as Christopher Colombus did, for the trade winds to take them to the West Indies. There are yacht marinas
In Tenerife: Real Club Náutico, Carretera de San Andres, Santa Cruz de Tenerife. Tel: 27 37 00.
In Gran Canaria: Real Club Náutico, Leon y Castillo, Las Palmas. Tel: 23 45 66.
In Lanzarote: Casino Club Náutico, Calle Blas Cabrera Felipe, Arrecife.
In Fuerteventura: Club Náutico Mar Azul, Puerto Azul Tarajalejo, Tuinje.
In Palma: New Royal Yacht Club, General Mola 6, Santa Cruz de la Palma, Tel: 41 11 84.
In Gomera: Yacht Club, Calle del Conde, San Sebastián de la Gomera. Tel: 87 10 53.

Places of Interest in the Eastern Canaries

Gran Canaria

Approximate distances are given from Las Palmas (capital)

Agaete 39 kms Picturesque small town in fertile countryside of north west.

Arguineguin 64 km Fishing village in the south; tourists, harbour, restaurants, bars, petrol, repairs, weekly market. Apartments and hostal. Small beach.

Arucas 17 km Centre of banana growing area; large town with imposing parish church, municipal park and gardens. Nearby Montana de Arucas, a volcanic cone, is good viewing point for coastline panorama.

Caldera Bandama 48 km Spectacular deep volcano crater 609 m above sea level, now green and peaceful. Nearby view point and golf course.

Fataga 65 km Attractive tiny village in valley between mountains on southern route from Tejeda. Palm trees, small bars, souvenirs, shops.

Galdar 40 km Old Guanche town, now commercial centre. Town hall interesting, Guanche relics, dragon tree. Nearby cave Cueva Pintada has geometric wall paintings.

Ingenio 27 km Eastern inland town, narrow streets, old houses. School of Needlework and Embroidery.

Jardin Canario 38 km Botanical gardens in beautiful green Angostura Valley. Free entrance.

Las Palmas, capital City, international port, noisy commercial centre, tourist resort. Two golden sandy beaches. Large hotels, apartments, restaurants, bars, nightclubs, discos. Old buildings, parks and churches.

Los Berrazales 57 km In Agaete Valley, lush vegetation, high green mountains, very scenic route 6 km of exotic flowers, shrubs and trees. Restaurant.

Maspalomas 60 km One of the most beautiful beaches 7 km long. Sand dunes, swimming, bars, hotels, apartments, souvenir shopping, camel rides, fishing, golf, old lighthouse.

Pinar de Tamadaba 66 km Gran Canaria's last primeval forest in the north west at 1300 m. Canary Fir trees more than 98ft/30 mts. A good road leads via Cruz de Tejeda to the heart of the forest, be careful not to get lost in the dense woodland.

Playa del Inglés 54 km The beach is over two and a half kilometres long and joins the Maspalomas sand dunes. Swimming, layout chairs, sun umbrellas, promenade. Restaurants, bars, hotels, apartments, bungalows, commercial centres, nightclubs, discos, entertainments, bright lights. Cheerful holiday resort, fun for all the family.

Puerto de Las Nieves 43 km Fishing village on west coast, two pebble beaches, swimming, fishing, Fish restaurants, souvenir shops.

Puerto Mogan 81 km Quiet fishing port in southwest. Fish restaurant, petrol, tropical fruits, local vegetables. Nine kilometres up scenic valley to village of Mogan in mountains, lush vegetation, restaurant, shops.

Pinar de Tamadaba 66 km Gran Canaria's last primeval forest in the north west at 1300 m. Canary Fir trees more than 98 ft/30 mts. A good road leads via Cruz de Tejeda to the heart of the forest, be careful not to get lost in the dense woodland.

Puerto Rico 71 km Man-made holiday resort in southwest, good sandy beaches, two harbours, yacht marinas, pleasure and fishing boats, deep sea sport fishing. Sea excursions, water sports, tennis, bowling. Many bars, restaurants, supermarkets. Tourist entertainment. Apartments, post office, banks. Popular place with good sunshine record.

San Bartolome de Tirajana 53 km Small pretty town at foot of mountains, palm trees, attractive houses, restaurant, views.

Tejeda 44 km Pretty little village, rural setting, almond and orange trees, petrol. Cruz de Tejeda is centre of island, panoramic views, bars, restaurant, souvenirs, donkey rides, National Parador.

Telde 14 km Busy commercial town, south of Las Palmas. Good market and interesting church.

Teror 21 km Set high in the mountains, a quiet Canary town with typical carved pine balconies. Old Canarian mansion open to the publis. Seventeenth century church. Hand-made lace.

Like most Canarian churches, the Señora del Pino at Teror has an impressive facade and an ornate interior that is welcome and restful for the tourist. It is the sanctuary for the alabaster image of the Virgin of the Pine.

Fuerteventura

Approximate distances are given from Puerto del Rosario (capital)

Betancuria 28 km Ancient island capital hidden away in lovely valley in western mountains. A national historic monument. Seventeenth century cathedral. Small village bar restaurant, souvenir shop, small ethnographic museum.

Caleta de Fustes 13 km Modern development on east coast, sandy beach, yacht harbour, apartments, sports facilities. Isolated.

Corralejo 38 km Important town on north coast. Alisur Ferry to Lanzarote. Pleasure and fishing boats, yacht harbour. Hotel, apartments, supermarket, shops, petrol, taxis, disco, restaurants. Nearby sandy bay, good underwater swimming, windsurfing.

Cotillo 39 km Remote north-west coast fishing village. Tourist development, sandy bays, rocks, good fishing, fish restaurant.

Gran Tarajal 48 km Second largest town and port. Grey sandy beach. Promenade, shops, restaurants, bars. Petrol, post office, banks.

Isla de los Lobos 38 km to Corralejo Small islet 2.5 sq kms north east of Fuerteventura. Day trips from Corralejo. Sandy beaches, swimming, restaurant. Peaceful.

La Oliva 24 kms Quiet historic inland town. Large parish church. Casa de los Coroneles, former governor's palace, now being restored. Casa del Capellan, old mansion, high wooden doors with Aztec design. Post office, shop, no restaurants.

Las Playitas 51 kms Small developing seaside village, sandy bay and pebble beach, fishing boats, bar. Attractive position 4 kms from Gran Tarajal.

Morro del Jable 100 kms Large village in extreme south of Jandia. Fishing boats, fish restaurant, shops, petrol, banks, supermarkets. Hotels at Jandia Playa.

Pajara 43 kms Inland town notable sixteenth century church with carved stone portal Aztec design. Peaceful country setting.

Parque Natural de las Dunes 28 kms Amazingly beautiful area of sand dunes on north-east coast. Wildlife, picnics, swimming, clear seas, naturist sunbathing. Hotels at northern end.

Playa Jandia 75 kms Southern peninsula of white sands and flat beaches.   Scattered modern developments south of Costa Calma. Splendid swimming, clear seas, sunbathing. Panoramic views, utterly peaceful, naturist area.

Puerto del Rosario Capital Town and port. Quietly interesting. Post Office, banks, shops, market, small restaurant, petrol, repairs. Headquarters of Spanish Foreign Legion. Nearby Playa Blanca beach undeveloped.

The palm lined Plaza de Santa Ana is always full of tourists and school children who delight in feeding the pigeons that flutter around. In the background is the handsome Town Hall.

Lanzarote

Approximate distances are given from Arrecife (capital)

Arrecife Capital Main port and busy, untidy, friendly town. Ancient fort. Hotels, apartments, shops, small market, restaurants, bars. Promenade, small sandy beach on edge of harbour, yacht club, sailing.

Costa Teguise 9 km East coast, designated for major residential and tourist development. Modern bungalows and apartments. Five-star Las Salinas-Sheraton hotel. Golf, tennis, swimming, sports clubs. Supermarket, small sandy beach at Los Charcos.

Cuevas de los Verdes 28 km In north, six kilometres of volcanic caves, many open to the public, conducted tour of passages once used by the Guanches.

El Golfo 32 km On south west coast, wide bay formed by volcanic crater, impressive strata, lagoon bright green from microscopic organisms. Pebble beach, rocks. Parking, no bars.

Haria 30 km Pleasant small town in north amid oasis of palm trees. Restaurants, bars. Agriculture, wild flowers. Mirador (2 km south) gives extensive views.

Jameos del Agua 30 km Underground cavern 225 m long, recently built theatre. Lagoon formed by infiltration of sea, in which are unique tiny white crabs. Marvellous decor, cactus, ferns and exotic plants. Bar restaurant, small swimming pool. Nightclub.

La Caleta de Famara 25 km Remote pebble, sand and shell beaches on north-east coast, small tourist development. Quiet fishing village, goats, simple small bar-restaurants.

La Graciosa (Orzola 37 km) Islet off north coast, dry trips from Orzola. Sandy beaches, water sports, fishing. Landrover tour of islet.

Los Pocillos 11 km Large sandy beach at edge of tourist area. Accommodation. Clear water for swimming.

Mirador del Rio 37 km Extreme north, high look out point and attractive modern restaurant. Good views of small islets. Car park.

Mozaga 1 km In centre of island at crossroads. Modern monument to honour peasants of Lanzarote, by Cezar Manrique. Museum and restaurant. Bodega for wine tasting.

Papagayo 40 km At southern tip, splendid beach but difficult access over sand dunes and dirt road. Worth the effort in suitable vehicle. No facilities on beach. Very tranquil setting.

Playa Blanca Sud 40 km Pleasant small village and port in south. Ferry for Fuerteventura, yacht harbour. Fish restaurants, supermarkets, guesthouse. Small beach, apartments and villas. Quiet.

Puerto del Carmen 15 km Centre of tourist activities, south east coast. Hotels, apartments, villas, shopping. Sports, entertainments. Happy family location.

Salinas de Janubio Large saltpans on south-west coast salt water lagoon, visited by migratory sea birds.

Teguise 12 km Old capital of island, in north central. Ancient church and historic buildings. Narrow streets. Nearby volcanic summit Guanapay. Sixteenth century fort, Santa Barbara.

Timanfaya National Park 34 km Most spectacular sight on island. Area of approximately 200 sq kms covered with lava rock and ashes from eruption. Fire Mountain trip includes demonstrations of steam and heat from ground, coach tour in strange lunar-like landscape. Camel ride up side of volcano. Restaurant. Very awesome and impressive.

Yaiza 23 km Southern island. Delightful tidy little North-African-style town, encased in black lava ashes. Church, tourist shops and restaurants. Colourful and interesting.

The small fishing village of Las Playas, where it is hard to tell between old and new buildings; so well do the past and present styles of housing blend together.

2 Where to stay

Accommodation in the Canaries ranges from luxury hotels to simple guesthouses and camping. In Tenerife and Gran Canaria the choice is vast. Lanzarote has increased the number of beds available to tourists, recently, but the development is being strictly controlled to suit the islands amenities. Fuerteventura has a new building programme in the south, but at the moment accommodation is not plentiful. La Palma, La Gomera and El Hierro have little tourist accommodation, except for the **paradors** there.

An up to date list of all types of accommodation currently available can be obtained from the Tourist Offices. For Tenerife, La Palma, Gomera and El Hierro the address is:
The Tourist Office (Palacio Insular), Plaza España, Sant Cruz de Tenerife. Tel: 24 22 27.
For Gran Canaria, Lanzarote and Fuerteventura:
The Tourist Office, Parque Santa Catalina, Las Palmas de Gran Canaria. Tel: 26 46 23.

It is recommended that you choose accommodation that has been inspected by the Tourist Board and that you book through property or travel agents. It is unwise to seek unlisted places, especially in the cities where some proprietors may not observe security regulations nor maintain hygiene standards.

Hotels and Guesthouses

Hotels (*Hoteles* — H) are classified from 1 to 5 stars. The rating is always displayed outside as H plus the number of stars. Hotels provide rooms and meals as required in their own restaurant. The larger hotels usually have outdoor swimming pools, tennis courts, shops and entertainment. Many have courtesy buses to take visitors to the beach. Those with three stars or more provide rooms with private bathrooms and toilets. Most have balconies often with sea views. Maid service and laundry should be available.

Hotel Apartments

Hotel Apartments (*Apartamentos Hoteles* — HA) are similar to hotels but have flats bungalows or chalets. The star rating is shown after HA.

Resident Hotels

These hotels (*Hoteles Residencia* — HR) supply rooms but without restaurant facilities. They usually have less luxurious furnishings though often have private bathrooms and toilets. Shown as HR with star rating.

Guesthouses

Modest hotels and guesthouses (*Hostales* — HS) with a star rating of one to three. They provide accommodation with or without meals. They do not have dormitories.

Pensions

Guesthouses (*Pensiones* — P) with a small number of rooms, providing full board.

Residences

These establishments (*Residencias* — R) provide accommodation with a shared bathroom. Breakfast only available.

Inns

Inns (*pousadas, tabernas*) are usually in country districts; the standard is mostly good, but can vary. It is best to view rooms before booking. Often in beautiful surroundings with local atmosphere.

Description of Star Rating

Five Star hotel Air conditioning in public rooms and bedrooms. All bedrooms have complete bathrooms, hot and cold water, telephone. Laundry and ironing service. Some suites have sitting rooms. Garage, lift and bar. Hairdresser.

Four Star hotel Air conditioning in public rooms and bedrooms. 75% of bedrooms have complete bathrooms, hot and cold water, telephone. Laundry and ironing service. Garage, lift and bar.

Three Star hotel Permanently installed heating. 50% of bedrooms have complete bathrooms. 50% have showers, washbasin, WC, telephone. Laundry and ironing service.

Two Star hotel Permanently installed heating. 15% of bedrooms have complete bathrooms, 47% have showers, washbasin and WC, one common bathroom to six bedrooms, telephone. Lift in buildings of more than four storeys.

The unusual circular building of a three star hotel in Playa del Inglés, conveniently situated near the centre of town and popular with British tourists.

One Star hotels   Permanently installed heating. 25% of bedrooms have washbasin, shower and WC. 25% with shower and washbasin. One common bathroom to every seven bedrooms. Laundry and ironing service. Telephone on every floor. Lift in building of more than five storeys.

Three Star guesthouses   5% of bedrooms with complete bathrooms. 10% with shower, washbasin and WC, one common bathroom to every eight rooms, telephone. Laundry and ironing service. Lounge.

Two Star guesthouses   All bedrooms have washbasin, one common bathroom to every ten bedrooms. General telephone. Lounge and lobby. Lift in five storey buildings.

One Star guesthouses   All bedrooms have washbasins with cold water. One bathroom for twelve rooms. General telephone.

It is advisable to book accommodation in advance, particularly at the time of Festivals and at tourist resorts. Reservations in writing can be sent direct to hotels. Letters sent to Five, Four and Three-Star hotels can be written in English. For lower categories it is advisable to write in Spanish.

More details of hotels are given in the description of each island. Some (approximate) non-package prices are:

Five Star — Las Salinas/Sheraton Hotel, Lanzarote
  Double room — 9000 pesetas (£46);   Full board — 3800 pesetas (£20) per person;   Breakfast — 550 pesetas (£3) per person;   Lunch or dinner — 2100 pesetas (£11) per person.
  15% service charge included. 3% tax not included.

Four Star — Arrecife Gran Hotel, Lanzarote
  Double room — 4500 pesetas (£23);   Full board — 1950 pesetas (£10) per person;   Breakfast — 250 pesetas (£1.30) per person;   Lunch or dinner — 1100 pesetas (£5.70) per person.

Three Star — Hotel Eugenia Victoria, Gran Canaria
  Double room — 2900 pesetas (£15);   Full board — 1425 pesetas (£7.40) per person;   Breakfast — 180 pesetas (92p) per person;   Lunch or dinner — 750 pesetas (£3.90) per person.

Two Star — Valeron Hotel, Fuerteventura
  Double room — 1200 pesetas (£6.20).

Three Star — Hotel Apartments, Playa del Ingles, Gran Canaria
  Double room — 3600 pesetas (£18.60)
  Full board — 1720 pesetas (£8.90) per person.

Two Star — Hostales Residencia, Estavez, Arguineguin, Gran Canaria.
  Double room — 1300 pesetas (£6.70)

Paradors

A **Parador** is the name given to hotels (Parador Nacionales de Tourismo) of State for Tourism in Spain and the Canary Islands. Usually they are in converted historic castles, palaces, convents and monasteries and generally in a location of special scenic beauty or interest. Internal decor is of a luxurious standard, often containing antiques and works of art. They offer every comfort as well as an excellent cuisine. The restaurants are open to non-residents. Sometimes paradors can be more expensive than equivalent hotels but they provide a unique tourist experience. It is advisable to book in advance.

The Spanish Tourist Office publishes an informative brochure called *Paradores,* which is given free on request. In the Eastern Canaries there are paradors in:

Gran Canaria — Parador Nacional de Tejeda: Two star Canary style modern building. 19 bedrooms, bar restaurant open to visitors. Splendid views, high altitude. Tel: 65 80 50. (Re-opening date not yet known.)

Fuerteventura — Parador Nacional de Fuerteventura: Three star modern building overlooking Puerto del Rosario and the sea. 24 rooms, swimming pool. Tel: 85 11 50.

Lanzarote — There is no Parador Nacional in Lanzarote.

Apartments and Villas

Self-catering accommodation is available on all the main islands. In the big resorts purpose-built blocks are of enormous size, having their own restaurants, public rooms, swimming pools, sports facilities, supermarket, haridressing salon and boutique. Some have evening entertainments, such as flamenco shows and music groups.

In the apartments (*Apartamentos*), basic provisions will include bed linen, towels, kitchen equipment and cooking facilities, with cutlery, crockery and glasses. The majority have balconies often with sea views. High rise blocks have lifts. Most provide maid service but in some cases only once a week.

At the reception, details will be found of local entertainment, coach excursions and car hire.

Bungalows and Villas

Often built around a swimming pool, bungalows and villas are more attractive as they usually have gardens and shrubs close by. There are always restaurants, bars and supermarkets in the vicinity.

Some (approximate) non-package tour accommodation prices are:

Puerto Nova, Puerto Rico, Gran Canaria — Luxury two bedroom apartment over looking harbour, can sleep six persons : 27,000 pesetas (£140) per week. Price includes welcoming pack of groceries. Public rooms, swimming pool, restaurant and bar. Maid service once a week.

Los Molinas, Costa Teguise, Lanzarote — Apartment or bungalow, can sleep four: 5830 pesetas (£30) each person per week; restaurant, bar, lounge and swimming pool. Studio for two persons; 3130 pesetas (£16) each person, per week; Extra bed 850 pesetas (£4.50) per week; cot 250 pesetas (£1.30).

Puerto del Rosario, the capital, where new apartment blocks are a growing feature of a town that is becoming increasingly modernised.

Travel Agents

There are numerous travel agents (*viajes*) in the tourist parts of the Canary Islands. Their services are varied; agents for hotels, apartments, ferry and flight bookings; car hire, coach tours and currency exchange. Open from 0900 to 1300 and 1630 to 1900 hrs, Monday to Friday. 0900 to 1300 hrs on Saturday and closed on Sundays and Public Holidays.

British run Viajes Blandy, Fernando Poo and Wagonlit Cooks have branches in Gran Canaria and Tenerife. Other well established firms are Viajes Cyrasa, Melia, Insular and Ultramar Express. The latter two firms have English-speaking staff and run many excursions throughout the islands with coaches that are modern and comfortable.

Viajes Insular, Gran Canaria: Luis Morote 9, Las Palmas. Tel: 23 31 44. Carretera General, Maspalomas. Tel: 76 05 00. Centro Comercial, Puerto Rico. Tel. 74 50 18. **Fuerteventura:** General Franco, Puerto del Rosario. Tel: 85 61 51. Playa de Jandia. Tel: 87 61 51. Playa de Corralejo. Tel: 86 61 01. **Lanzarote:** Avenida de la Mancomunidad 30, Arrecife. Tel. 18 13 55. Centro Comercial, Playa Blanco. Tel: 82 52 08.

Ultramar, Gran Canaria: Calle Luis Morote 37, Las Palmas. Tel. 27 27 10. Edificio Mercurio, Avenida Tirajana, Playa del Ingles. Tel. 76 10 00. **Fuerteventura:** Complejo Stella Canaris, Jandia. Tel. 87 61 68. Apartementos La Oliva, Corralejo. Tel. 86 62 47. **Lanzarote:** Centro de la Penita, Puerto del Carmen. Tel. 82 60 08.

The recently modernised fishing harbour at Arguineguin is a pleasantly level area for the meeting of many motorcaravanners who like to swop news and information, as well as doing their shopping at the colourful outdoor market held there every Tuesday.

Camping

Camping rules that apply in mainland Spain also apply in the Canary Islands. A copy of the camping regulations should be obtained by anyone intending to camp in the Canaries. This can be obtained from:

The Spanish National Tourist Office 57-58 St. James's Street, London SW1A 1LD. Tel: 01 499 0901.

The official list of camp sites in Spain shows only two sites in the seven Canary Islands. Both are in Gran Canaria. There are still no official camp sites in Tenerife, though it is reported that a project to open a camp site at Mesa del Mar, between Puerto de la Cruz and La Laguna, is underway and has Town Hall approval. It is also reported that plans are afoot for a camp site in La Palma, but nothing is yet confirmed. Because of the lack of camp sites, off site camping is tolerated in the islands, but care is required in conforming with the regulations.

It is not necessary to have a Camping Carnet, but it is an advantage, particularly for those who camp outside sites, as third party insurance is included. Camping Carnets can be obtained from camping and motoring organisations such as the AA, RAC and Caravan Club, and cost approximately £1. A passport-size photo is required.

Camping on site

You will be required to present your passport at the camp site reception. Persons under the age of 16 may not be admitted unless accompanied by an adult. Silence must be respected between 2300 and 0800 hours. Fires are not permitted except in allocated places. Campers are not allowed to carry offensive weapons. Valuables may be left with the camp manager for safe keeping. Most sites have their own post boxes and supermarkets. Every reception office has an official complaints book.

As we said above, the official list of campsites in Spain shows only two sites in the Canary Islands, both in Gran Canaria. During the winter of 1982/83 the site shown as at Temisas was closed; no information is available if or when it will reopen. Effectively, the only official campsite in the Canaries at present is Camping Guantanamo, a Class 3a site, owned by a local Canarian who lives in Las Palmas. In fact the camp consists of three separate sites.

The original **Guantanamo Camp One** is situated on the sea-side of the main Puerto Rico to Mogan road and managed by Senor Santiago and his family, plus their large friendly, alsatian dogs. They live on site and all take much interest in the campers' welfare. Used mainly by 'backpackers' and 'tenters', it has some permanent caravans owned by Canarians; there are also a few 'cells' for rent. These are just bare rooms that can be locked; no beds are provided and they can be booked in advance.

On the camp the facilities are sparse. Basins and showers have cold water only (but with the climate being so pleasant this is not a great hardship). Sinks are provided for dish and clothes washing. Open wood fires give communal cooking facilities. Toilets are adequate, except when the camp is crowded, usually at Christmas time. Recently a supermarket and bar restaurant have been built adjoining the main road.

The restaurant is under separate management and service is of a high standard with a friendly atmosphere, delicious food and an interesting menu. Price of a main course is about 450 pesetas/£2.30. It is open to non-campers.

Tents are pitched on very hard ground. Some are sited in the shade under trees or straw awnings, other places are without shade. Predominantly, a younger type of camper uses Camp One. Parties and 'sing-songs' are organised amongst themselves. The beach, which runs around a horse-shoe bay, is a mixture of sand and pebble and suitable for swimming. At one end are two bars, and adjoining the camp, on the beach, is a small shop with a verandah where campers may enjoy a drink, or sit and watch the sunset.

Camp Two is across the main road, opposite Camp One, behind high concrete walls with gates that are closed at night. Tents are not allowed, though awnings attached to caravans and motorcaravans are permitted. marked pitches are sheltered by tall trees and the camp is swept clean every day.

A modern toilet block has cold showers, basins for washing, laundry and chemical toilet disposal. Electric points are available (220 volts) and the power is on from 1800 to 2300 hrs. Several times a week Senor Paco arrives in his huge Mercedes van selling an assortment of locally grown fruit and vegetables, eggs and groceries. Those who have been at the camp for several of the winter months feel he is very much part of their life. It must be pointed out that this camp becomes very full over the Christmas period.

Camp Three is located about 3 kilometres inland, along the valley (*barranco*) in an unusual and attractive setting, with dry volcanic mountains on three sides — a sheltered situation. This site, opened in autumn 1982, is very level and clean and, provided one does not mind a venue a few miles from the sea, it makes a pleasant and peaceful place to camp. Here both tents and vans are allowed.

The site is managed by Geraldo and Geraldine, helpful and hardworking Canarians who have lived in London and speak English. It has a small bar, among tall eucalyptus trees, with tables and chairs outside. The modern toilet block has wash basins and cold showers (which in mid-afternoon are nicely lukewarm from the sun). Electricity is available from 1800 to 2300 hours. But the pride and joy of this camp is the good-sized swimming pool, which is also a splendid place to sunbathe. Cheerful Geraldine cooks a tasty meal for you either at midday or in the evening and will smile with delight when you tell her how much you enjoyed her paella or steak and chips. Grilled sole, wine and coffee for two cost us 915 pesetas (£4.70).

For all three camps, minimum booking is for six days. Price for two persons, car, caravan and electricity is 2500 pesetas (£13) per week. For one person and a tent, 1000 pesetas (£5).

Camping off site

Camping is allowed outside official camp sites provided one has the permission of the owner of the land. Areas where most campers tend to congregate are in the south of Tenerife and the south of Gran Canaria but, generally speaking, campers are accepted on all the islands (although Canarians would prefer that visitors used the hotels, villas and apartments). We advise campers to seek the advice of the local police when they wish to camp in this way.

No more than three units may camp together for more than three days outside a site and the number must not exceed ten persons. In the case where campers wish to stay longer, special permission must be obtained, giving at least 15 days notice, from:

Provincial Delegado de Turismo calle de la Marina 5, Santa Cruz de Tenerife. Leon Y Castillo 17, Las Palmas, Gran Canaria.

Camping is not allowed in the following places:
— on dry river beds, seasonal flooding areas; — within military, industrial or tourist areas; — within a radius of 150 metres from

the source of a town's water supply; — within urban areas or unreasonably near the roadside; — within one kilometre of an official camp site.

Backpackers
As we have said, although there are many beaches, camping is not permitted in most tourist areas. In the past, the 'hippy' type of backpacker has caused the authorities much trouble: hence the reluctance to let groups of campers forgather. However, backpackers do visit the islands, using simple hostels with the odd night camping; but care is required in conforming with the regulations.

Caravans
The terrain of the Canary Islands is not conducive to touring with a towed caravan, therefore these mostly go to the camp at Tauro, Gran Canaria; or after using them to cross Europe, their owners stay at a rented villa or apartment. A few hardy caravanners may find quiet places which are suitable for a short stay, having obtained permission from the police or the owner: these sites, usually on waste ground, are few and far between.

Motorcaravans
Certainly the most suitable way to camp in the Canary Islands is to use a motorcaravan. The diversity of scenery and regions makes travelling interesting and varied. Provided one parks with consideration to the regulations there should be few problems.

Hints for campers
One of the main requirements of all campers is water, which, in the Canary Islands, is in short supply. Therefore it is necessary to conserve and plan ahead. Most petrol filling stations will allow containers to be filled but make sure that it is drinking water (*agua potable*) or buy bottled water from a supermarket. Camping 'Gaz' is available in towns and some villages.

Further information on camping in the Canary Islands can be obtained from periodicals such as *Caravan; Camping; Motorcaravan and Motorhome Monthly; and Motorcaravan World.*

A newly formed club for caravan and motorcaravanners has recently been formed in Tenerife. One of its aims is to improve camping conditions and amenities on the islands. Further information can be obtained from:

Tim Wise, Apartado 174, Edificio La Palmera, Puerto de la Cruz, Tenerife. Tel: 37 13 38.

Package Holidays

There are many UK firms operating package holidays to the Canary Islands. These provide a wide choice of selection and offer good value to holidaymakers with a limited amount of time. They also enable customers to budget in advance for most of their holiday expenses.

When you book a package holiday, the price of the air fare is included, plus transport to and from your destination, unless otherwise stated. Tour operators' brochures will give details of flight arrangements, type of resort, entertainments and the star rating of the accommodation. These vary from five-star luxury hotels to modest guesthouses, self-catering apartments and villas. In some instances it is possible to visit more than one island during your holiday.

At present the islands of Tenerife and Gran Canaria have the most package tours available, with Lanzarote a very popular third choice. Fuerteventura has recently entered the tourist market and now has hotels in both the north and south. Only one tour operator, Scotia, use La Palma. Gomera and El Hierro are not at present included in package holiday programmes, but no doubt it will happen in due course.

In the larger resorts and holiday complexes like Puerto de la Cruz, Tenerife and Playa del Inglés, Gran Canaria, entire hotels and apartment blocks are taken over by the tour operator and prove so popular that they are full for most of the year. The cheaper high season packages are to simple self-catering apartments and cost about £225 per person sharing a double room or apartment for two weeks. Hotels will cost about £275 to £350 for the same period but can increase to £500. (One has to remember that the Canary Islands are a 4½-hour flight from London, which makes it more expensive than going to the Mediterranean.)

Amongst the tour operators offering Canary Island packages are:

Airways, Blue Skies, Cambrian, Carousel, Cosmos, Ellerman, Enterprise, Flair, Global, Intersun, Lanzarote Villas, Lanzotic Travel, Mundi Color, Portland, Scotia, Silvair, Sovereign, Student Travel, Thomas Cook, Travel Club, Tjaereborg, Thomson Holidays, Wings, Yorkshire Travel.

Saga Holidays offer package holidays for the 'over 60's', to Tenerife and Gran Canaria during 'off peak' periods.

Property and real estate agents

The Canary Islands present an appealing location for purchasers to invest in property, but it is advisable to get specialist advice on the subject.

Selling apartments, bungalows and villas, the administration of properties, letting, legal advice, repairs, technical services and insurance, are all transactions carried out by real estate companies in the Canary Islands, and most of the firms employ multi-lingual staff, trained to assist clients.

'Time sharing' is on the increase and firms like Wimpey have recently entered the market. Urbanizaciónes, as property developments are called, tend to group in nationalities in particular areas. For instance, Scandanavians seem not to mix a great deal with Germans.

The British appear to favour Puerto de la Cruz and Playa de las Americas in Tenerife. Gran Canaria has British residents in the Tafira district of Las Palmas, in Playa del Inglés and Puerto Rico. A big proportion of British residents like Lanzarote where English is well understood.

Real estate companies and agents where English is spoken are:

Gran Canaria — Imobiliaria Roca, Avenida Maritima del Norte Las Palmas Tel. 21 65 00

Agencia Zabolota, Reloj 2, Las Palmas Tel. 31 49 22

Lanzarote — Lanzarote Villas, 37 East Street, Horsham, Sussex, UK Tel: 51304

3 Getting About in the Canaries

There are no trains in the Canary islands so you have to get about by road. Fortunately the main roads and motorways are good, and *autopistas* (motorways) are free of tolls. Traffic is only heavy in cities and towns but the driving is well disciplined. However roads in the country are sometimes little more than rough tracks across desert land and progress can be slow.

A good road map of the Canary Islands is therefore essential. Recommended is the series published by Firestone Hispania available in the Canary Islands from petrol filling stations and bookshops. In Great Britain and Ireland they can be obtained from bookshops with a strong foreign map section or direct, by post, from the agent, Roger Lascelles (Dept Firestone) 47 York Road, Brentford, Middlesex, TW8 0QP. Tel: 01-847 0935.

Map Ref	Description
T-32	Canary Islands
E-50	Tenerife
E-51	Gran Canaria

Driving in Spain and the Canary Islands

If you are taking a car to the Canary Islands, driving through Spain and taking the car ferry from Cadiz to either Tenerife or Gran Canaria you will require the following:
1 Driving Licence
2 International Driving Permit
3 Green Card Insurance (your insurance company issues)
4 Bail Bond (from AA, RAC or insurance company — this is an indemnity if you are involved in an accident).
5 Vehicle Registration Document
6 Passport
7 A spare set of light bulbs (Spanish law requirement)
8 A red triangle, for warning of breakdown obstruction.
9 Means of changing direction of headlight dip.
10 GB sticker

Up to date information on this subject is best obtained from the AA, RAC or the Spanish Tourist Office. However, the following points are worthy of note:

- Drive on the right-hand side of the road.
- Sound your horn when overtaking.
- Stop for pedestrians on crossings.
- Wear seatbelts.
- Sidelights only required in built up areas.
- Do not cross the single white line, it is equivalent to the double white line.
- Observe the no overtaking signs, and speed limits.
- Give way to traffic coming from the right, particularly at roundabouts.

Road signs

Most road signs are international. One important traffic control is the *cambio de sentido* (change direction), generally controlled by traffic lights, which prevents vehicles turning across oncoming traffic or from doing a U-turn. Here are some road sign translations:

Aduana   customs post
Aparcamiento   parking
Atencion   caution
Blancones   soft verges
Cedo el Paso   give way
Despacio   slow
Desvio   diversion
Derecha   right
Escuela   school
Estacionamiento prohibido   no parking
Izquierda   left
Obras   workmen
Pare   stop
Peligro   danger
Peligroso   dangerous
Paso prohibido   No throughfare
Peatones   pedestrians
Salidas   exit

Petrol Filling Stations

In the Canary Islands petrol filling stations are closed all day on Sundays and public holidays. They do not provide car repair services; this is a separate service, *taller mechanico*. Good toilets and drinking water can be found at filling stations. Autoshops sell spares and sweets. Car wash services are similar to those in the UK.

At the time of writing petrol is 68.8 pesetas (35p) per litre. It comes in three grades: Extra — 98 octane, Super — 96 octane, Normal — 90 octane. Do not confuse petrol (*gasolina*) with diesel.

Car Servicing and Repairs

There are plenty of places for servicing and repairing cars. The cities of Tenerife and Gran Canaria have agents for most well-known British and foreign cars. There could be some delay in obtaining a particular spare part required from abroad.

In country places a small workshop (*taller mechanico*), which deals with local vehicles, will assist. The standard is good and repairs are promptly effected. Costs are usually more reasonable than in the UK. Facilities for tyre fitting, battery charging and car washing are available.

Car Hire (Self drive)

Car hire agencies in the Canary Islands include international names like Hertz and Avis, Organización Canaria Coches Aquiler (abbreviation OCCA) and local firms. Prices vary, so it is worth shopping around if you are in a large resort like Playa del Ingles, Gran Canaria or Puerto de la Cruz in Tenerife.

The type of cars range from a luxury Mercedes to a safari jeep. Motorcycles, scooters and bicycles can also be rented. (Crash helmets have to be worn on motorcycles.) Some idea of price is given (clients pay for petrol):

Seat 133	1600 pesetas (£8.24) per day
	9100 pesetas (£47) per week
Seat 127	1900 pesetas (£9.80) per day
	13300 pesetas (£68) per week
Seat 132	4000 pesetas (£20) per day
	23100 pesetas (£119) per week
Renault 4TL	1700 pesetas (£8.70) per day
	9800 pesetas (£50) per week
Mazda 323	2750 pesetas (£14) per day
(automatic)	17150 pesetas (£88) per week
Micro bus	4150 pesetas (£21) per day
(Volks)	27930 pesetas (£144) per week

An area that is designated for future tourist development in the south, Costa Calma, has miles of golden sands — let us hope that it will live up to its name!

In some instances the minimum age for drivers is 21. Passport, driving licence and a deposit of about 7000 pesetas (£36) are required. Confirm that vehicle insurance is included in the hire cost — this is usually about 350 pesetas (£1.80) per day and personal insurance 150 pesetas (77p) per day.

It is advisable to book in advance.

There is an on-the-spot fine of 1000 pesetas (£5) for failing to use seat belts. Maximum speed in towns and villages is 40 kph, elsewhere 90 kph. Police patrol on motor cycles especially on the Carretera General (main road).

Taxis

Taxis are a pleasure to use on the Canary Islands and give a good but not always cheap service. Generally they are large Mercedes and kept very clean by their Canarian drivers. You may have to listen to taped Canarian music and some drivers do not allow smoking. At night most display a green light as being available for hire, also there is a sign indicating 'free' (*libre*). Taxis in the larger towns have meters and the drivers are very good at giving change, though they expect a tip (*propina*] of about ten per cent.

For those taxis that do not have meters, or if you wish to go beyond the city or town limits, it is necessary to arrange the price beforehand. Misunderstandings usually occur because of lack of communication, some drivers will write down the price and place, which is helpful. Baggage may require a surcharge of about 20 pesetas (10p) per item.

Typical fares (at time of writing):
- Santa Cruz de Tenerife to Reina Sofia (airport) — 3000 pesetas (£15.50)
- Las Palmas de Gran Canaria to Airport — 700 pesetas (£3.60)
- Las Palmas de Gran Canaria to Playa del Ingles — 2600 pesetas (£13.40)
- Las Palmas (city centre) to Port — 100-400 pesetas (51p-£2.06), depending which docks.

Tartanas (Horse Drawn Carriages)

In Las Palmas de Gran Canaria, horse drawn carriages are to be found on the Calle Simon Bolivar, opposite Plaza Santa Catalina. These gaily decorated open carriages allow you to view at a slow pace the seafront, docks, market and city centre.

A one-hour drive for four person costs about 600 pesetas (£3) though price should be previously arranged. A tip is expected.

Getting About by Bus

Gran Canaria and Tenerife are well provided with public bus services; in the other islands the service is adequate. Bus stops are marked, sometimes by *Parada* (stopping place). You always enter a bus from the front and buy your ticket from the conductor or or driver; only single journey (*ida*) tickets are issued. Remember to retain your ticket as inspectors cover all routes. Canary bus queues are usually orderly and line up facing the direction in which the bus will travel. For long distances there are fast buses having limited stops, sometimes marked *Expres* or *Directo.* Buses run every day including Public Holidays. Timetables can be obtained from Tourist Offices and some bus terminals. Further information is given in the sections describing individual islands.

Vehicles range from comfortable long distance coaches to ancient old bone-shakers. The Canarians call their buses *guaguas* pronounced 'wah wah' but *autobus* is generally understood.

Gran Canaria

Bus routes are centred on Las Palmas de Gran Canaria. City buses run from Parque Santa Catalina. The airport service starts from the Iberia Office, Calle Leon y Castillo, and country routes run from the bus terminal at Calle Rafael Cabrera, near the Parque de San Telmo.

Fuerteventura

In the capital, Puerto del Rosario, the buses leave from the Calle Alfonso 13. The north route goes to Corralejo via La Oliva; the central route to Betancuria and Pajara; the route to the south via Antigua to Gran Tarajal and Morro Jable.

Lanzarote

The bus terminal in Arrecife is on the Calle Garcia Escaures. Main routes run in three directions: north to Teguise and Maguez; a central route to Tinajo and Soo; south to Yaiza, Puerto del Carmen and Playa Blanca.

Excursions by Coach

Some examples of the cost of coach tours from Gran Canaria, Lanzarote and Fuerteventura:

Gran Canaria
• Tour round the island, starting from the south, full day, 1,500 pesetas (£7.75)
• Jeep safari into the mountains, full day, 1,200 pesetas (£6.20)
• Sioux City, Wild West film set, half day, 850 pesetas (£4.40)
• Wild West night, barbecue, entertainments, evening, 2,250 pesetas (£11.60)
• A day on windjammar 'San Miguel' from Puerto Rico, full day, 1,900 pesetas (£9.80)

Lanzarote
• Tour of island including lunch, full day, 2,500 pesetas (£12.90)
• Tour of south and volcanic route, including lunch, full day, 1,975 pesetas (£10.20)
• Canary festival night, including food 1,850 pesetas (£9.50)

Fuerteventura
• Tour of island, including lunch, full day, 1,600 pesetas (£8.20)
• A day at sea including food, 1,500 pesetas (£7.75)
• Visit to Isla de los Lobos, including food and swimming, full day, 1,500 pesetas (£7.75)

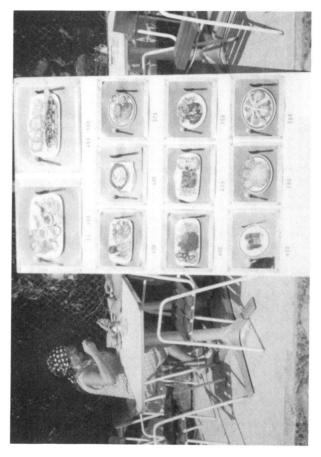

This is a daily menu, Canarian style. The pictures of dishes available, with their prices enable tourists with little Spanish, to see what there is to eat and make their choice.

4 Food, Drink and Entertainments

Food

The Canary Islands, because of their duty free ports, have a great variety of food and drink. The tourist areas, especially, are full of exotic foodstuffs from all over the world. Santa Cruz de Tenerife and Las Palmas, Gran Canaria, with their international traffic, offer an enormous selection of gourmet and epicure foods.

Prices of imported foods from Spain tend to be higher than on the mainland. Most other food prices are comparable with, if not cheaper than, Europe. Of course, if you buy a tin of baked beans with an English brand name, then it will be more expensive than a similar product bearing a Canarian or Spanish brand name.

Meat (*carne*) is plentiful. Local Canarian pork (*cerdo*) is excellent: pork chops (*chuleta de cerdo*) are on every menu. Beef (*carne de vacca*) is of good quality and imported from Brazil. There is no problem with getting it minced (*carne picada*). Lamb (*cordero*) and mutton (*carne de carnero*) are rather more expensive. Liver (*higado*) and kidneys (*rinon*) are cheap and tasty. Chickens (*pollo*) are plentiful, fresh or frozen. Very succulent is young goat or kid (*cabrito*) which is roasted on special festive occasions. Rabbit (*conejo*) is much used for stews.

Fish (*pescado*) is found in all towns and villages, though sometimes supplies run out early in the day. Prices are high owing to the demand. Varieties include, tuna (*atun*), cod (*bacalad*), hake (*merluza*), swordfish (*espada*), mackerel (*caballa*) and sardines (*sardinas*). It is possible to go to the fishing villages and buy fish straight off the boats but the prices remain high.

Cheese (*queso*) is imported from many countries and Dutch cheese can be bought more cheaply here than in Holland. Goat's cheese (*queso blanco de cabra*) mainly from the smaller islands, is particularly flavoursome.

Milk (*leche*) is not often sold fresh, as there are few cows on the islands. Most milk is 'long-life' imported from Holland in cartons or plastic containers. Tinned and powdered milk are also available.

Bread (*pan*) is sold in most supermarkets, but the place to buy really fresh bread, including brown, is a baker's shop (*pana deria*). Rolls and bread are light but not crusty as French bread. Cakes may be bought from a *pasteleria*. These do not usually sell bread as well, but have a selection of sweets and chocolates (*confites y bombón*).

Various brands of tea and coffee are on sale, including ground coffee and Nescafé, the latter a little dearer than in the UK. Excellent local and Spanish honey (*meil*) can be bought, the date palm honey (*meil de palma*) has an unusual flavour.

There is plenty of fresh fruit and vegetables. This is best bought in the open markets but supermarkets in the tourist centres are well supplied. The selection is wide, so enjoy fresh strawberries and pineapples at Christmas time!

Local Dishes

It is possible to have typical British meals in the Canaries. 'Real English Breakfast' signs are displayed in all tourist resorts. Most hotel restaurants serve food that tends to be bland; trying to please all their customers, they refrain from too much flavour.

Local dishes often include *papas arrugadas* (wrinkled potatoes) — quite delicious little new potatoes cooked in their skins in sea- or salt-water; these should be eaten with their skins on. Served with chops or fish, they will be accompanied by a Canarian piquant sauce called *mojo,* made of oil, vinegar, salt, pimento and spices. *Mojo picon* is red and hot, *mojo verde* is green and milder; often the sauces vary according to the cook. The sauce can be obtained in supermarkets, a small bottle costing about 70 pesetas (36p).

Familiar Spanish dishes include *gazpacho* — a tasty cold soup made from tomatoes, onions, pimentos, olive oil and sherry; and *paella* — rice cooked with saffron to which is added meats, fish and vegetables. *Tortilla* can be a simple omelette or *tortilla española* when potatoes, onions and vegetables are added.

Canarian soups (*sopa*) are tasty and almost a complete meal, so many good things are included. The one that is recommended to tourists is *sopa de berros,* watercress soup with herbs.

Stews (*puchero* or *estofado*) are considered a main dish; often made with rabbit (*estofado de conejo*), they are eaten with *gofio,* a meal made from wheat or maize which is toasted before being ground, and then made into a sort of dumpling, or sometimes eaten as bread.

Fish stew (*cazuela canaria*) is a fish casserole, with potatoes, onions, tomatoes, peppers and saffron. Sometime the fish is cooked whole, the vegetable juices being served first as a soup, then the fish and vegetables are eaten. Try some *pulpo* — better forget that it is octopus, then you will enjoy it!

Chicken (*pollo*) is usually roast (*pollo asado*) on a spit and will be served with chipped potatoes, these can often be offered as 'Take away' meals.

Deserts (*postre*) are usually fresh fruit (*fruta*), ice cream (*helados*) or *flan* which is a crème caramel. Mouth watering *gateaux* are filled with strawberries (*fresas*) and cream (*nata*).

Other island specialities are *quesadilias* — cheesecakes from El Hierro, and *rapaduras* — an almond and honey sweet from La Palma.

Our special favourite Canarian foods are:

Cabrito al horno	— roast young goat
Cochinillo asado	— roast suckling pig
Cocido canario	— Canarian stew
Cordornices rellenas	— stuffed quail
Jamón canario	— local ham
Parillada criollo	— charcoal steak
Salmonetes fritos	— fried red mullet
Atun con salsa de tomate	— tunny fish in tomato sauce
Zarzuela	— fish stew
Plátanos a la canaria	— banana fried in brandy sauce
Galletas de almendra	— almond biscuits

Drink

All the islands produce their own wine but in such small amounts that there is little for the visitor to buy. The best is said to be *vino del monte* from Gran Canaria. Lanzarote's *Malvasia* or malmsey wine is in better supply; it can be bought sweet (*dulce*) or dry (*seco*). Tenerife produces a *malvasia* and a *moscatel,* El Hierro has a *vino dulce,* a sweet wine. La Palma's wine is also a *malvasia* and can be purchased sweet or dry. The latter is pleasant when chilled and served as an aperitif.

Plenty of wine is imported from mainland Spain and sells from 70 pesetas (36p) a litre. Good Spanish wines come from Rioja, Valdepenas and Jumilla. Spanish champagne costs from 194 pesetas (£1) per bottle.

The local drink is rum (*ron*) which is distilled throughout the islands and sold in every bar and supermarket. It is a fiery spirit which needs to be tasted with caution. *Ron Miel* is a honey rum, similar to a liqueur. As you would expect there is a drink made from bananas: this is a yellow liqueur called *cobana*. Other liqueurs are produced from oranges, pineapples, cherries, almonds and coconuts; assorted bottles of these liqueurs make attractive souvenirs.

As liquor is duty free it is cheap; even whisky is less expensive than in Europe or at duty free shops in airports or ships. It is possible to buy English beer from a keg; however the local beer (*cerveza*) is a light cool drink which is very refreshing at all times. Mineral waters and soft drinks such as Coca-cola and Seven-up are plentiful. The latter drink can be helpful if you have a queasy tummy.

Spanish brandy (*conac*) is said to have a less delicate flavour than French brandy. 'Soberano' and 'Fundador' are two Spanish brandies that are 37° proof, costing about 340 pesetas (£1.75) per litre, it is worth tasting. 'Sangria' is a Spanish drink, popular with tourists, that is usually served in a jug for two or more people. It is a mixture of red wine, orange juice, brandy, mineral water, slices of fruit and plenty of ice — refreshingly cool, it can be more potent than it tastes.

Tipping

Tipping (the *propina*) is expected, as in the UK and the Continent. In bars, cafes and restaurants, even though a service charge may be added, a tip in the region of ten per cent is generally given, perhaps less for a drink at the bar. The Spanish are proud and well-mannered and do not make much of the subject.

Porters, maids and cloak room attendants should also be tipped 10 or 25 pesetas, though porters at airports may have a fixed charge per piece of luggage. Taxi drivers expect a ten per cent tip.

Bars and Restaurants

In bars it is not necessary to pay for your drinks until you leave, even if you are there all day or night. They never close until the last party leaves. Tipping (called *propina*) is usual. The Spanish eat canapés or appetisers (called *tappas*) when they have a drink; sometimes these are quite elaborate, almost a meal. Lunch is served in restaurants between 1300 and 1500 hrs and dinner from 1930 to 2230 hrs.

It is quite in order for unaccompanied females to use cafés, bars and restaurants. Girl students often sit in a cafe with a coffee for an hour or so studying their books. Friends will meet at a table in the sunshine for an aperitif, drink a glass of wine, eat some olives or peanuts, and no one will hasten their departure. The end of the afternoon is the time when women take a cup of chocolate and *churros* — delicious sweet fritters, freshly cooked. Black coffee is *café solo,* white coffee is *café con leche.*

Tourist offices have lists of recommended restaurants and local newspapers have plenty of advertisements. The choice of type of restaurant or bar is enormous, nowhere could a greater variety of cuisine be enjoyed. Both Tenerife and Gran Canaria have establishments of the very highest international standard. The range goes down to the very sleazy bars in the red light districts of the cities.

All restaurants in the Canary Islands must display a tourist menu of the day *menu del dia,* at an average price of 450 pesetas (£2.50); sometimes this includes wine. The menu might be a substantial soup, grilled steak or pork chop, salad, fried potatoes, bread, ice cream or cake. Coffee is always extra. As on the continent, in the Canary Islands food and drink consumed at the bar is cheaper than when ordered from a waiter (*camarero*) and served at a table.

Restaurants are graded into four categories, denoted by the number of forks (*tendores*) shown. The grading reflects the price rather than the quality of the food, with four forks being the highest grade.

The best way to sample local food is to eat where the Canarians gather. Do not be shy of entering, the islanders are well used to seeing tourists about, mostly they take little notice and just get on with their own lives.

Out of town the bars and shops can be unobtrusive, often having half closed doors with maybe a faded coca-cola sign. Once inside the service will be friendly but not inquisitive.

Restaurants — Gran Canaria (South)

Restaurants — Canarian

El Papá Dulce, C.C. Nilo.
Gorro Blanco, San Fernando. Tel: 760465.
Grill El Guanche, Cita. Tel: 761638.
Las Cubas, San Fernando.
Mercurio Vega Vega, Maspalomas (Playa del Inglés).
Tenderete II, Avda de Tirajana. Tel: 761460.

Restaurants — Chinese

Bali, Apts. Tinache. Tel: 763261.
China, Apts. Dunubio/Avda de Italia. Tel: 760323.
Chino Oriental, Cita. Tel: 261055.
House Ming, Jardin del Atlantico.
Hong Kong, Adva de Espana.
Pekin, Cita. Tel: 761068.
Shangrila, Edifico Excelsior.

Restaurants — Dutch

Broodje van Toon, Cita-Oben.
Los Arcos, Bung. Los Arcos. Avda. Estados Unidos. Tel: 761833
Snack Corner Holland, Edif. Iguazu, Local 8.

Restaurants — French

Anno Domini, C.C. San Agustin. Tel: 762915.
Sancocho-Gourmet, Sun Club.

Restaurants — German

Alstadt Düsseldorf, Cita. Tel: 762630
Bier Brezl, Cita. Tel: 760437.
El Canario, Cita.
Düsseldorf, Cita.
Frankfurt, Kasbah. Tel: 760346.
Futterkrippe, Cita.
Maritim, Avda Sargentos Prov.
Zum Roten Kater, Cita. Tel: 760791.

Restaurants — International

Atlantic I, Kasbah.
Balconclub, Apt. Balconclub.
Bamira, Apts. Bamira, San Agustin.
Biarritz, Avda. de Bonn.
Boccalino, Hotel Don Gregory.
Buenos Aires, Avda de Espana.
Don Alejandro, Europlace.
Don Luis, Cita. Tel: 761949.
Don Pedro, Avda Estados Unidos 9.
Drago, Aguilo Roja.
Dunasol, Lisboa 3.
El Puente, Las Flores, San Agustin. Tel: 762400.
El Veril, Hotel Parque Tropical. Tel: 760512.
Emily, Kasbah.
Eurogrill, C.C. Gran Chaparral.
Europa, Avda Alfereces Prov. Tel: 760591.
Gofio Grill. Sun Club.
La Colina, Morro Besudo San Agustin.
La Epoca Gatsby, Cita.
La Petit, Aguila Roja.
La Rôtisserie, Apt. Corona Roja. Tel: 760656.
La Rotonda, hinter Hotel Tamarindos, San Agustin.
Las BraSAS, Avda de Tirajana.
Las Faluas, Avda de Tenerife 9.
La Toja, Apts. Barbados.
Lenamar, Apt. Lenamar.
Minirestaurant El Veril, CC El Veril. Tel: 762957.
Monte del Moro, San Agustin.
Monte Rojo, Sunwing, San Agustin.
Parque del Paraiso, near Kasbah.
Puerto Chico, Playa de Las Burras, San. Ag.
Saint Tropez, Avda de Alemania 4. Tel: 760763.
Santa Barbara, Bung Santa Barbara, Calle Barcelona.
Santa Monica, Apts. Santa Monica. Tel: 761966.
Sol y Sombra, Kasbah. Tel: 760102.

Restaurants — Italian

Chez Mario, Nueva Europa. Tel: 761817.
Giorgio, Cita.
Pinochio, Sandia, Italian.

Restaurants — Pizze

Berlin, La Rotonda. Tel: 761034.
Capri, Cita.
Cita Pizza, Cita.
Dixi, Apts. Corona Blanca. Tel: 761608.
El Padrino, Cita. Tel: 761044.
Loopy's Pizzeria.
Luigi, Sandia. Tel: 761188.
Mainz, Patalava III. Tel: 735844.
Mamma Mia, Edificio Barbados I.
Pizzeria Dixi, Corona Blanca, Playa del Inglés. Tel: 761608.

Restaurants — Spanish

La Cabana, San Fernando.
Carlos V, Cita.
Del Torero, Apts. Corona Roja. Tel: 760355.
Del Torero, Corona Roja. Tel: 760355.
Doramas, Gran Chaparral.
El Paleto, Cita.
El Tango, C.C. Nilo. Tel: 762381.
El Toro Negro, Kasbah.
Fayna, Avda. Estados Unidos.
La Chabola, Cita.
La Cohera, Sandia.
La Estancia, Cita. Tel: 762788.
La Estrella de Oro, San Cristobal de La Laguna. Tel: 762849.
La Paella, Alf Provisionales. Tel: 761131.
Las Lanzas, C.C. Gran Chaparral.
La Perla, Cita. Tel: 761626.
Lauria, Cita.
Los Colegas, Aguila Roja.
Los Mariachis, Avda. Gran Canaria.
Meson El Gallego. Avda. Gran Canaria.
Meson del Gitano, Playa de Las Burras.
Meson Viuda de Franco, Caretera General. Tel: 760371.
Niko, C.C. Aguila Roja.
Padaban, Kasbah. Tel: 760499.
Planeta Azul, Apts. Tanife. Tel: 760319.
Polaris II, Sandia.
Pulpo de Oro, Edif, Koka.
Sancho Panza, Morro Besudo. Tel: 760026.
San Fernando, San Fernando. Tel: 760980.
Taberna Gallega, Hotel Rey Carlos. Tel: 760332.

Villanueva, Gran Chaparral. Tel: 761046.

Restaurants — Steak

Berlin, Metro. Tel: 762386.
Bistro, La Sandia. Tel: 760480.
Condor, C.C. La Sandia.
El Gaucho, Aguila Roja. Tel: 761114.
Kentucky Grill, Sandia.
La Taba, C.C. Aguila Roja.
Loopy's Tavern, Las Retamas, San Agustin. Tel: 762892.
Lord Nelson III, San Agustin. Tel: 762083.
Paco & Tony, San Agustin.
Steakhouse Belgica, Aguila Roja.
Texas Grill, Playa de San Agustin.

Restaurants — Various

Pfeffermühle, Cita. Tel: 760685. Bistro/grill/int.
Beach Club San Agustin, Playa de San Agustin. Tel: 760370. De Luxe.
Lido Restaurant, Paseo Costa Canaria. De Luxe.
Lord Nelson II, Avda de Tirajana. Tel: 762250. De luxe.
Moby Dick, Aguila Roja. Fish restaurant.
Chichis, Apt. Taidia. Fish specialities.
Los Aguacates, Apto. Aguacates. Tel: 762683. Flambées.
KOKA Restaurant, Apts. KOKA. Fondue.
Buganvilla, Los Jazmines (San Agustin). Gourmet.
Rocas Rojas, San Agustin. Gourmet/intern.
Pam Pam Steakhouse, Aguila Roja.
La Pampa Linda, Playa de Las Burras. Tel: 761888. Grill.
Rincon, Cita. Grill.
Tibor, Cita. Grill flambé.
Budapest, Cita. Hungarian.
Café Susi, Cita. Konditorei.
Café Wien, Cita. Konditorei.
Lawrence of Arabia. Apts. Habitat. Tel: 763174. Oriental food.
Paella & Sangria, C/C San Agustin. Tel: 763030. Paella/ Gourmet.
Tango, Centr. Com. Nilo. **Restaurant-Grill.**
El Greco, Gran Chaparral. Tel: 761225. Sateh-bar.
Café de Paris, Hotel Ybarra Don Miguel. **Self-service.**
Las Camelias, Avda. de Tirajana. Tel: 760236. Self-service.
Regente, Morro Besudo. Self-service.
Don Quijote, Cita. Snack bar.

Las Pampas, Cita. Tel: 762582. South-am. grill.
Avda de Gran Canaria, 121. Specialities.
Tessiner Stube, Cita-Keller. Swiss specialities.
Bodega Rondo, Apts. Rondo. Tel: 760320. Tapa-bar.
El Poncho, Apts. Rondo. Tipico espanol.

Fiesta in the Canarias is a time of much celebrating, with dancing and
music. All tourists are encouraged to join in the cheerful festivities.

Night Life

There is plenty to do in the evenings if you are in any of the big holiday resorts and especially the capital cities. You will find night clubs, casinos, discos, theatres, cinemas, bingo halls, bowling alleys and flamenco shows.

It is well known that the term night club (*sala de fiesta*) means a place where a wife or girl friend can be taken; often it includes more than one show, flamenco and folk dancing included. The shows in a cabaret are usually of a less innocent character.

Discoteca are the usual discos with flashing lights, modern music and a small dance floor. A few have free entrance but generally it costs about 400 or 500 pesetas (£2 — £2.50) and includes the first drink; further drinks will cost the same price. Discos open about 2200 hrs and last until 0300 hrs.

Another form of evening entertainment are the many night excursions by coach. Often these start from one of the hotels and journey into the mountains to a *ranchero* for a barbecue. The inclusive price will allow for some free drinks and a generous dinner, entertainment and dancing to a live band. Singing on the coach ride home is not compulsory! Other evening excursions include visits to night clubs with tables being reserved, a free first drink and dancing between shows.

A popular evening entertainment is to go to a Wild West Show: informal and fun, you can walk about a 'western town' (an old film set), under a starry sky visiting the 'jail house' or the 'old corral'. Exhibitions of daredevil horse riding, cattle drives and knife-throwing are intermingled with a huge barbecue meal and free drinks.

It is well to remember that eating out at night starts late, 2000 hrs onwards, with some restaurants serving meals until 0200 hrs. A number of restaurants provide music with dancing continuously throughout the evening. Often entertainments such as flamenco and folk groups have star appearances. An average price of a meal without drinks, in such an establishment could be 1000 pesetas (£5). Because of the warm nights the general trend is to stay out of doors much later than in the UK. Eating, drinking and dancing under the stars are very much part of Canarian night life.

Sports and Pastimes

Because of the mild climate and the proximity of the sea it is possible to participate in a wide selection of sports. Good facilities are provided on the major islands. The Canarians enjoy all forms of leisure activity and keep themselves very fit.

Land sports

Archery can be enjoyed in the grounds of a number of hotels.

Billiards is played in many hotels and bars on the island; tourists are welcome.

Bowling alleys will be found in all the tourist areas and cities, often with 12 fully automatic tracks, and smaller ones in some hotels. Very popular with the Canarian youth.

Bridge clubs exist in the cities and the game is played in most hotels. The British Clubs in Las Palmas, Gran Canaria and Puerto de la Cruz, Tenerife have keen members who welcome visitors.

Bullfights, In Tenerife the bullring is on the Rambla de Generalisimo Franco in Santa Cruz. In Gran Canaria it is 4 kms south of Playa del Ingles. Travel agents and hotels display posters when bullfights take place. Admission is usually about 900 pesetas (£4.50).

Canary wrestling (*lucha canaria*). The oldest and most typical of Canary sports, with traditions rooted in early history long before the Spanish conquest. It is a carefully preserved sport which young Canarians participate in with great keeness. *Lucha Canaria* is played by two teams of twelve wrestlers (*luchadores*). A special ring of 9 m diameter is used with a thick layer of sand to prevent injuries. The wrestlers go barefoot, dressed in shirt and shorts, the purpose of the fight is to floor one's adversary. Canary wrestling is incredibly popular, and boys start to learn at the age of three and carry on until about thirty five. Every town and village has a team and there is much rivalry. There are many grips and kicks to be learnt, all very technical. It is advised that visitors do not participate in this particular sport. Tourists can see the wrestling at fiesta time.

Camel safari The camel is used for working in the fields for part of the day. The rest of the time he is expected to take squealing tourists for rides. Maspalomas in Gran Canaria and the Fire Mountain in Lanzarote are the best places to have your camel ride. The camels, which are technically dromedaries, have wooden seats on which two people sit, one on each side of the animal. Not for the faint hearted, for the animal gives a great lurch as it gets off its knees! The movement is pleasing providing one can relax and not knock one's back against the hard seat. An exhilarating experience for the adventurous.

Chess (*ajedrez*) is often played in the open air; one of the best places to play or watch the game is in the Plaza Santa Catalina, Las Palmas, Gran Canaria. You can sit down and play at a chess table for as long as you like, provided you are not defeated.

Cock fighting is permitted in all the islands. In Las Palmas, Gran Canaria fights take place between December and May. Admission is free and the event lasts for about two hours. The tourist office has details.

Donkey safari Donkeys are still used as beasts of burden in the country. Nowadays they also have to toil up mountains with excited tourists astride their backs. Visitors are taken to a ranch and allocated a suitable beast, then in convoy they trail among the cactus and palm trees. It can be a hilarious outing for all the family, with guitar music, singing and plenty to eat. Details are advertised in hotels and travel agents.

Flying Sports airfields are found in Tenerife, Gran Canaria and Lanzarote. Visitors can have the opportunity to see the islands by air. Advance booking is necessary. Aircraft like the Cherokee 180, which takes three passengers are used. Information from Tourist Office or travel agent.

Football This game comes top of the popularity polls. In every small village a space has been cleared for a football pitch. Local teams compete in an inter-island league. The big stadiums are in Las Palmas and Santa Cruz, who are in the Spanish League.

Go-karting is a very new sport to the islands. A Go-Kart centre has been constructed about 5 kms north of Playa del Ingles, Gran Canaria. Open daily from 1000 to 2300 hrs, for adults and children; there are four kinds of Kart. There is a bar-restaurant.

Golf There can be few places in the world where this sport can be played in such original surroundings: on a volcanic crater and in a desert — both these courses are on the island of Gran Canaria. Other courses are situated in Tenerife and Lanzarote. Open to visitors, clubs and caddies available. Green fees are about 600 to 800 pesetas (£3 to £4) details from:

Campo de Golf, Maspalomas, Gran Canaria. Tel: 762581.

Greyhound racing takes place at night in the Canadroma, Playa del Ingles, Gran Canaria. Admission is free and there is a bar and restaurant. The standard of racing is good. Commencing at 2000 hrs from Tuesday to Saturday, 1800 hrs on Sunday, closed on Mondays. There is an electronic betting system and an English translation explains the betting rules.

Hang Gliding There are week-end flying courses, with expert tuition at:
Escula Tamaran, Leon y Castillo 244, Las Palmas, Gran Canaria.
The sport is also practised at Los Cristianos, Tenerife.

A sea safar is a pleasant way to see the coastline. The cruise includes swimming and catching fish for the barbecue lunch, which is enjoyed with a glass of sangria.

Ice skating There is a rink in Gran Canaria and ice skates may be hired.   Palacio de Hielo, Avenida de Escaleritas 31, Las Palmas, Gran Canaria.

Keep fit classes and programmes for physical training, jogging, judo and karate are organised in some of the larger hotels, especially those run by Germans and Scandinavians who are particularly keen on physical fitness and run large sports programmes for holidaymakers.

Mountain and hill climbing are enjoyed in Tenerife and Gran Canaria.   In Tenerife the Tourist Office will give information and literature describing walks on Mount Teide.   The owner of the Hotel Tigaiga in Puerto de la Cruz sometimes leads parties of walkers high into the Canadas, Mount Teide.   The Refugio de Altavista is a modern cabin which is an ideal overnight stop to enable climbers to see the dawn on Mount Teide.

In Gran Canaria the National Delegation of Youth organises walks and rock climbs.   There are two mountain refugees and sometimes arrangements can be made to hire equipment.
National Delegation of Youth, Plaza del Cairasco, Las Palmas, Gran Canaria.

El Oasis Horse Riding, near Faro, Maspalomas, Gran Canaria. Open 0800 to 1800 hrs.   Also camel rides.

Squash courts are to be found in some of the larger hotels.

Tennis is a much practised sport amongst the Canarians and tourists.   Public tennis courts are part of most of the modern tourist complexes;   with the warm nights many are open until late at night, being floodlit.   Most large hotels have tennis courts and coaching is available.
Cita Tennis Club, Avenida de Francia, Playa del Inglés, Gran Canaria. Tel: 761483.

Walking The Canary Islands offer a splendid variety of scenery and terrain for walking.   Miles of golden sands enable barefoot exercise.   Inland treks require stout shoes for much of the land is stony and very hard.   Remember to take a map if you venture off well-known routes, as distances can be very deceptive, especially if one intends to climb along the gorges (*barrancos*) or over the mountains.   Another warning;   there is very little evening and dusk falls quickly between 1800 and 1900 hrs.   Best to check with a local person before you set off on any long walk and let someone know which route you intend to go.   Take some rations, a compass and a hat — it's great fun walking in the islands, if done with caution.

Fishing is sometimes done at night but beforehand much must be discussed.

Water sports

Nautical activities abound around the island, for the warm sea temperatures greatly encourage beginners and experienced water sports people to indulge to the full.

Fishing comes naturally to Canarians who spend many hours of their spare time with a rod. Often they are contributing to the family diet. Most tourist places have jetties, harbour walls, rocks and beaches suitable for fishing. Rods, tackle and bait are for sale. Boats with rods may be hired from a number of fishing ports and villages.

Deep sea fishing The waters around the islands are noted for big game fish and every year fishermen from all over the world return to Puerto Rico, Gran Canaria for international competitions. Many record catches have been made in these waters.

Sport fishing is expensive for the demand is high. The cost to charter a boat and crew is about 20,000 pesetas (£103) per day, sometimes the owners will do a split charter for less. Boats are of a high standard and powerful. Great excitement is felt when around 1600 hrs each afternoon, these fast little boats return to harbour, their tough captains chewing a fat cigar with great nonchalance, while admiring tourists gasp with wonder at the huge fish. Marlin, tunny, shark, swordfish and barracuda are the big ones, with mackerel and sardines being used as bait.

Diving The seas around the archipelago have interesting underwater volcanic rock formations. Coral barriers and marine life make sub-aqua diving and swimming a fascinating pastime. Beginners courses in sheltered harbours, and boat excursions to interesting sites, are arranged. Aquamarine, near Arguineguin, Gran Canaria has full scale equipment for a sea film and photographic school. Cameras and lights can be rented. Cost of diving excursions starts at 1,200 pesetas (£6).

Sailing Every island, except El Hierro, has a yacht club. Many Canarians own either a sailing or motor yacht. The sport is very much on the increase and new yacht marinas are being developed. Water sport schools are big business in the tourist resorts, frequent outings are arranged for all classes of sailors and beginners. The International Sailing School, Puerto Rico, Gran Canaria, speak English and welcome visitors. A number of tourists take boats by trailer to the islands, especially in the winter season. Details of sailing schools and events are advertised in hotels and the local paper. All types of boats are for hire.

Swimming The Canarian beaches (*playas*) offer interesting swimming all the year round with the sea temperature never really cold. El Hierro, Gomera and La Palma are rather short of good beaches. The other four islands have a wide choice; golden sands, black sands, fine pebbles and rocky pools, always with lovely clear water. Seas are mostly calm, but remember this is the Atlantic, and big rollers can soon blow in, turning a tranquil sea into a fury of white foam and pounding breakers. Undercurrents around rocky areas can sometimes be dangerous. In tourist resorts a red flag is flown when bathing is considered unsafe by the lifeguards. Some of the best beaches include Teresitas in Tenerife, Playa del Ingles in Gran Canaria, Playa de los Pocillos in Lanzarote and the wonderful stretch of almost deserted sand at Jandia in the south of Fuerteventura.

Public swimming pools are found in Santa Cruz de Tenerife and elsewhere. All the big hotels, apartment blocks and villas have outdoor pools including smaller ones for children.

Water Ski schools are mostly found in the southern parts of the islands where the waters have a lower swell. Courses for beginners and more experienced water ski enthusiasts are well advertised in shops and hotels.

Windsurfing This fascinating sport is rapidly gaining immense popularity around the coasts. Many visitors arrive with their own boards on top of vehicles. Wind surfing can be a bit more tricky than it looks and professional advice is given on many beaches. Learning in sheltered waters helps to give confidence. A five-hour basic course costs about 2350 pesetas (£12). Experienced windsurfers can hire boards for 400 pesetas (£2) an hour. If it is all too difficult do not despair, you can always hire a *pedallo* (pedal boat) for 300 pesetas (£1.50) per hour — for two!

Sea excursions

Fun can be had by taking a sea excursion, bookable from hotel, travel agents or on the quay. Boats leave Gran Canaria and Tenerife most days full of cheerful tourists enjoying the sea breezes and improving their suntans (don't forget hats and sun tan oil).

There are 2½ hour trips or half-day cruises along the coast. Full-day outings will include food, drink, entertainment, music and swimming from the ship. A six-hour excursion may include catching a shark. Types of vessel can be small motorlaunches, larger motor cruisers or genuine old sailing ships. Costs are roughly:

2½ hour 'Sea Safari', including barbecued fish and wine, 700 pesetas (£3.60).

Full day excursion including food, drink and entertainment, about 1,400 pesetas (£7), children under ten half price.

Genuine old sailing ships take holidaymakers on an all day excursion. All aboard are encouraged to be crew members and assist with the big sails.

5 Practical information for holidaymakers

Time

Time is the same throughout the Canary Islands, and from the end of October to the end of March, it corresponds with the UK; the rest of the year it is one hour behind.

Electricity, Radio and Television

Electric current voltage is 220 to 225 AC, occasionally 110 to 125 AC. Plugs are the two round-pin variety.

There are local radio stations in the Canaries. News in English and other languages is broadcast daily. The World Service of the BBC is on short wave. It is possible to hear Radio 4 on long wave, when atmospheric conditions are good.

British television sets are not suitable in the Canary Islands. (Spanish television uses Norma G for black and white and Pall for colour.) Most hotels and many bars have black and white or colour television, and nearly all the programmes are in Spanish and relayed from mainland Spain.

Newspapers and Books

English daily and Sunday newspapers can be purchased in cities, tourist complexes and at airports, usually a day after publication. Newspapers are about twice the UK price. English books and paperbacks are also available in these places.

In Tenerife an English language newspaper *Here and Now,* is published on the 14th and 28th of each month. It contains lively information on hotels, eating places, news of events, topical subjects and advertisements, useful for the tourist as well as residents. Price 40 pesetas (21p). There is also a monthly magazine in English, for holidaymakers and residents, the *Island Gazette.* It is a well-established glossy magazine, nicely put together with news and views, up-to-date local information, including where to go and what to do. There are classified advertisements. Price 75 pesetas (38p).

Gran Canaria has a newspaper called *Canarias Tourist*, which is written with English, Dutch, German and Scandinavian translations. There are eighty pages crammed with information for the holidaymaker; it is recommended.

Published monthly, obtainable from bookshops and supermarkets, 150 pesetas (77p).

Taking Children to the Canary Islands

Taking young children to the Canary Islands presents no real problems. The Canarians are always interested in children, and indeed look after their own with much love and care.

Hotels, apartments and bungalows have cots and highchairs, sometimes at a small extra charge. Play rooms and paddling pools, plus babysitting services, help to make life pleasant for all. There are plenty of toy and clothes shops, baby foods and toilet requirements.

Amusements, train rides, playgrounds, ice creams, beach equipment, all are reasonably priced. Young children are allowed into bars, cafés, restaurants and hotel lounges until late at night. Hotels have courtesy buses to convey you to the nearest beach.

However, care should be taken not to overtire young children, who easily become exicted and possibly restless with the change of surroundings. New foods may not appeal but usually staff are understanding and helpful. Do not overdo the amount of fresh fruits or salads at first. Plenty of liquid to drink is sensible.

Young children often go on coach excursions and have a happy time. Do take some toys or games to amuse a toddler, for sitting in a coach will become tedious without some diversion. Use the toilet when the coach makes a stop for this purpose; drivers have to work to a schedule and it is not always possible to make emergency halts on narrow mountain roads.

With plenty of beaches and warm sea water most youngsters are completely happy. Please do not force your child into the sea, use a little encouragement to paddle or sit at the edge, it is not sensible to be 'tough' when a child is nervous of water. Making a sand castle and fetching a bucket of sea water will do a lot towards gaining confidence. Be sure to provide the child with a sun hat and protection for the skin, and do not leave him to play in the sun for too long at a time. Guard carefully against sunburn and sunstroke (see Health section).

Health

There are no dangerous animals or poisonous reptiles in the Canaries, not many flies and only a few mosquitos. The spring-like weather is healthy and invigorating. Over indulgence with food and drink can cause discomfort and an upset tummy. It is wise to wash all fruits and salads before eating.

There is no shortage of medications in the Canary Islands, but if you prefer a particular British brand it is wise to take a supply with you. Tap water should not be drunk by visitors unless it is first boiled. Water considered fit for drinking is *agua potable* and unsuitable is *agua non potable*. Bottled water is quite cheap and available at supermarkets: called *agua mineral* it is either aerated (*con gas*) or still (*sin gas*).

Canary tummy is a form of sickness and diarrhoea which may last for a few days. Take 'Salvacolina' a suitable Spanish medication, for this, available from chemists. Should the complaint persist it is advisable to consult a doctor. However cases of upset tummy are not to be expected and most people find the Canary climate will make them feel years younger.

Care should be taken to avoid too much initial exposure to the sun. The wearing of sun hats and sun glasses can be helpful. Remember that the sun's rays are very much stronger here than in the UK, so allow periods of fifteen minutes exposure to direct sunlight, at first, to parts of the body not usually exposed. Make sure that plenty of sun lotion is applied. Do not wait until the skin is turning red, that may be too late.

Sunstroke can be very distressing. Symptoms are a severe headache, vomiting and much discomfort. Mild cases require a cool shaded room with plenty of liquid. ('Seven Up' is a helpful drink.) Apply calamine or similar cream to affected parts. If the skin is blistered or the symptoms are not improving, do not hesitate to consult a chemist or doctor. Hotels have the addresses and telephone numbers of the nearest doctor or clinic.

Doctors

Doctors (*médicos*) have clinics which are run in a business-like manner. In tourist resorts, there would be an English speaking receptionist. You usually get immediate attention and pay a fee of about 2000 pesetas (£10) for a visit or consultation. They will give you a receipt for insurance purposes. If you are given a prescription you take it to a chemist (*farmacia*) whose sign is a green Maltese Cross. Unlike in the UK, chemists in Spain sell only medications, not toilet requirements, but they are able to give you advice and first aid.

There are also First Aid Posts (*Casa de Socorro*), which is a national service. These posts are often in the country and the buildings are marked with a red cross and a road sign.

Dentists

Dentists (*dentista*) are fully qualified, similar to doctors. The service is good and not over expensive. Generally one can call at the surgery, without an appointment, and take one's turn.

Opticians

Opticians (*optica*) provide a very good service. In towns and tourist centres they are able to test your visions, without charge, and supply the required spectacles in about 48 hours. Generally charges are lower than in the UK, with a very good choice of frames.

Medical

Spain is not in the EEC as yet, therefore medical and hospital expenses have to be paid for. In the case of hospitals, operations usually have to be paid for in advance or guaranteed, so it is wise to take out insurance to cover this eventuality before leaving the UK.

Gran Canaria

Hospital Insular, Avenida Maritimar del Sur, Las Palmas. Tel. 31 30 33.
Ambulance, Las Palmas. Tel. 24 05 23.
Clinica, Playa del Inglés. Tel. 76 27 42.
Clinica, Puerto Pico. Tel. 74 57 47.
Red Cross (Cruz Roja), Las Palmas. Tel. 24 44 06; Maspalomas. Tel. 76 28 81.

Fuerteventura

Ambulance, Puerto del Rosario. Tel. 85 03 12.
Red Cross, Avenida Almirante, Carrero Blanco, Puerto del Rosario. Tel. 85 12 76.

Lanzarote

Hospital, Juan de Quesada, Arrecife. Tel. 81 05 00.
Clinica Gonzalez Medina, Garcia Escamez, Arrecife. Tel. 81 13 24.
Red Cross, Coronel Valls de Torre 24, Arrecife. Tel. 81 06 32.

Public Conveniences

Public conveniences are few and far between in the Canary Islands. They are marked *aseo* or *servicio. Senoras* (ladies) and *Caballeros* (gentlemen). Pictographs are also used. Toilets are available at petrol filling stations. It is quite permissible to use the cloakrooms of a hotel, bar or café and it is not necessary to be a customer.

Public conveniences will be found in market (*mercado*) places, but they are sometimes austere. Payment for the use of a toilet is not required but it is usual to tip the attendant 5 pesetas.

The Casa de Los Coroneles (The Colonel's House) at La Oliva, inland towards the north end of Fuerteventura.

Communications

Post

Post Offices (*Correos*) similar to those in the UK are in all towns and some villages. Open from 0900 to 1300 hrs. Monday to Saturday, closed on Sunday and Public Holidays.

You may have letters and parcels sent to a local post office for you to collect. They should be addressed to you (Surname first, then initials) at Lista de Correos, in the appropriate town (e.g. Lista de Correos, Puerto Rico, Gran Canaria, Canary Islands, Spain). There is no charge for this service. When you collect your mail from the post office you will be required to show your passport.

In shops where you purchase postcards, stamps are usually sold as well. At the time of writing postage to the UK for a letter costs 33 pesetas (17p) and for a postcard 23 pesetas (12p). All mail goes by air; parcels can be registered.

The Canary Island post boxes are painted yellow, similar in shape to those in the UK. The exception is at main post offices where posting boxes are in the walls of the building. Sometimes they are marked *extranjero* (for posting abroad) and *insular* (for local islands). Small yellow post boxes, square in shape may be attached to houses in remote country villages.

Telephones

Telephoning from the Canary Islands to the UK or other countries is simple, provided the coin box is not too full to accept further coins. This happens quite frequently in busy tourist centres. Look for a telephone kiosk which says *international;* those marked *urbano* are for local calls only.

You can use 50, 25 or 5 peseta coins, and the directions for use are displayed in several languages near the telephone. In hotels, the switchboard operator will dial your number for you and call you back as soon as the call is through. Some hotels have telephones in the bedroom. A small charge is made for this service.

When using the public telephone, first dial 07 for international calls. Wait for a high pitched continuous sound then dial the code of the country required (for UK this is 44) followed by the subscriber's code and number. In cases where the code starts with 0 it is omitted. For example, for London (01), just dial 1.

International country code numbers from the Canary Islands:-

Austria	—	43
Denmark	—	45
Germany	—	49
Holland	—	31
Italy	—	31
Portugal	—	351
Sweden	—	46
UK	—	44

Cost indication, UK — 87 pesetas (45p) per minute.

By dialling 9198, it is possible to arrange personal calls. *Cobro revertido* means the recipient of the call pays the cost.

For general information concerning telephones, telegrams, cables and telex, dial 003.

Telegraph

Cable messages can be passed, day or night, by way of the main telephone exchange. Dial 362000.

Telex

For teleprinter service, dial 363717.

For emergency remittances, one's own bank at home can send money by teleprinter to a Spanish bank. This service can be granted very quickly. If necessary, ask permission to use a travel agent's telex.

Home is as near as your nearest telephone! A generous allocation of conveniently sited public payphones is a feature on all the islands.

Money

Currency and banks

The Canary Islands are a part of Spain and therefore the currency is the *peseta*. The coins in use are: 1, 5, 25, 50, 100 peseta. Notes are: 100, 500, 1000, 2000 and 5000 peseta.

The 'high street' banks there are the same as in Spain and have names like, Banco de Bilbao, Banco Hispano Americano, Banco de Santander and Banco Central. Opening hours do vary slightly but generally are 0930 to 1400 hrs daily, closing at 1300 on Saturdays. Closed on Sundays and Public Holidays. Most Spanish banks accept Eurocheque cards or equivalent, displaying the sign. Be sure to check with your own bank whether your cheque card is valid for use in Spain (the Canary Islands). When you go to the bank you will need to take your cheque book or traveller's cheques, and your passport, they will probably wish to know where you are staying. One can also cash traveller's cheques and exchange currency in travel agents and hotels. The currency exchange rate is displayed in most banks and travel agents. At the present time it is 194 pesetas to £1, for cheques. A small commission is charged for the transaction. Our experience is that the Banco de Bilbao gives very favourable rates of exchange, accepts Eurocheque cards and has English speaking staff.

The larger hotels will have deposit boxes or small safes for guests to lock up their valuables. The Canarians generally are law abiding but in busy plazas, markets and at fiesta time it is sensible to take precautions against pickpockets.

Budgeting for your holiday

The cost of living should not prove higher in the Canary Islands than Europe or the UK. Generally speaking, package tour holiday-makers require spending money for entertainments, drinks and possibly additional meals, unless the package includes full board. You must allow for extra costs such as taking part in sports and excursions, the hire of chairs and sun umbrellas, laundry, and tips (*propina*) for waiters, taxi drivers and porters (about 10%); and maybe some extra film for the camera and souvenirs.

Prices in tourist areas will probably be a few pesetas higher than elsewhere but if one takes into account the extra cost of travelling to a non-tourist area to do one's shopping, it will probably work out much about the same. For the independent traveller, it is possible to live quite cheaply especially by buying local foods. Chickens, tomatoes, cucumbers, eggs, bread and many drinks are less expensive than in the UK. Bars and restaurants are less costly and give a cheerful and good service.

Shopping

Shopping in the Canary Islands is very much like shopping in the UK and Europe. Even in the smaller islands there are the supermarket-type shops with prices marked on all goods. In the tourist areas the shop assistants will understand English but their knowledge of German will be even better, owing to the higher percentage of tourists coming from Germany..

Shopping baskets and trolleys are available, any personal parcels of shopping may have to be deposited at the entrance, and a numbered tag is given as a receipt. In some shops you are expected to select your own vegetables. Sometimes meat is prepacked but usually at the meats, fish, cheese and delicatessen counters you are served. It may be necessary to take a numbered ticket for order service.

Amongst the many good buys in the Canary Islands are embroidery, ceramics, palm leaf baskets, wood carvings, colourful costume dolls and cigars. Because so many items are imported duty free (no tax), certain goods can be cheaper here than in the country of origin. Tobacco, liquor, cameras, radios and watches can be purchased with a saving in cost.

All the big towns and many villages have open air markets, where the atmosphere is friendly and informal. The markets are a good place to start a conversation with the Canarians, who are outgoing friendly people. When Canarians go shopping they like to socialize; rarely do they expect to be served without having a chat.

Churches

The Canarians are mostly Roman Catholics and have churches in all towns and villages. Visitors are always welcomed with courtesy

Anglican and Evangelical Churches are to be found in the main tourist resorts. Lists of addresses with times of services can be obtained from Tourist Offices and large hotels. There are no synagogues in the Canary Islands.

Churches in Gran Canaria

(Anglican) Holy Trinity Church, Calle Rafael Ramirez, Las Palmas, Gran Canaria.

(Baptist Evangelical) Ingeniero Salinas 17, Las Palmas, Gran Canaria.

Problems and Complaints

Complaints about accommodation should be made an official complaints forms (*Hojas de reclamaciones*); tourist establishments should have these or the Tourist Office will provide them.

Usually the receptionist or the public relations representative (*relacions publico*) will be glad to sort out your query, they generally speak english. In extreme cases it may be necessary to go to the police (*policia municipal*) or the Town Hall (*Ayuntamiento*). You will find officials pleased to assist, but be patient; the Canarian way of life is not to hurry.

Consulates

In case anything untoward should happen like losing your passport, it is useful to know the whereabouts of the nearest Consul. Police Headquarters and the Town Hall (*Ayuntamiento*) will also assist. Information notices and books in hotels are handy places for finding such addresses.

British Consulate in Gran Canaria Alfredo L. Jones 33, Las Palmas. Tel. 26 25 08.

American Consulate in Gran Canaria General Primo de Rivera 5, Las Palmas. Tel. 27 12 59.

Police Las Palmas. Tel. 20 23 22.

Police

There are several types of police in the Canary Islands and Spain. The *Guardia Civil* who wear a green uniform with a shiny black hat, are armed law enforcement officers. It is advisable not to get involved in a misunderstanding with them, they rarely admit to speaking English and have a great deal of power. The Municipal Police are the local town and village police, either in brown or dark blue uniforms. The Traffic Police, besides controlling traffic, give assistance with breakdowns and other problems. Their patrol cars are marked *Tráfico Policia*. All types of police are approachable and helpful, especially the Traffic Police.

Fire precautions

Fire precautions are observed in the Canary Islands, with public buildings and hotels being inspected for adequate fire escape equipment. Details of emergency exits are shown in each hotel room. Modern fire fighting equipment is located in all places of population.

Clothes

You will need lightweight clothes for the Canary Islands. A heavy top coat is not necessary but windcheaters, anoraks and woollen jumpers are essential when visiting high mountain areas. A lightweight raincoat may prove useful.

Generally speaking, loose-fitting cotton and drip-dry garments are the most comfortable. For walking in the hills take stout flat-heeled shoes, as the terrain can be very hard and stony. On the beach rubber flip-flop sandals are useful. Remember that one's feet tend to swell in warm weather so take light footwear.

Sunhats and sunglasses should be used, for the sun in the Canaries is strong and care must be taken to avoid sunstroke.

Evening wear is mostly casual. Some hotels and restaurants require men to wear ties and jackets. When visiting churches it is not essential to wear a hat or scarf but it is expected that you will not be wearing beach clothes. Skimpy clothing is frowned on in towns. Some banks and petrol stations will refuse to serve you if you are not adequately covered.

On beaches bikinis are permitted and topless sunbathing is seen. Notices are displayed in the few places where naturists may take off their clothes, such as Maspalomas Dunes in Gran Canaria.

Buying clothes locally

When in Tenerife, Gran Canaria and Lanzarote you will be able to purchase any clothes you may require from a good selection of shops. The main tourist resorts have plenty of boutiques with modern styles. Men's and children's clothes are available, too, in all styles and sizes.

Prices cover a wide range. Many of the Paris fashion houses have shops here and the big stores have whole floors full of all types of clothing including sportswear. Bargain counters with cheaper goods will be marked *rebaja* which means a reduction in price. Sometimes the open air village markets have good bargains but examine the goods to see that they are not shop-soiled.

Being a duty free area it is possible to find oriental silks, furs and leather goods at advantageous prices. When possible it is a good idea to check on the equivalent UK price first.

The range of clothes in the shops of La Gomera, La Palma, El Hierro and Fuerteventura is more restricted. However it is possible to buy various materials and have clothes made up. In Las Palmas or Tenerife a gentleman's suit can be tailored in 24 hours.

Clothes imported from Spain can be a little more expensive. Marks and Spencer have a small branch in Las Palmas, Gran Canaria, with clothes being slightly more costly than in the UK. Most of the hotels have a boutique nearby; the local supermarket will probably stock beachwear, sportswear, lightweight shoes and hats.

The local hand-embroidered blouses, skirts and shawls make attractive souvenirs. Prices vary little between the various islands.

Laundry

If you wish to have clothes cleaned or laundered, it is probably easier to use the services of your hotel or apartment. Maids will collect laundry and return it clean the same day, lists of charges are usually put in each room. Dry cleaners are more rare and very busy. Launderettes are only just beginning to appear in the major tourist resorts.

With the warm sunshine clothes dry very quickly so drip-dry garments are practical. There are all the usual washing powders and detergents available.

Hairdressing

Men's barbers are called *barberia* and ladies' salons *Peluqueria.* In tourist areas prices are higher than in towns. Most large hotels have their own salons and the standard is generally very good. The Canarians have particularly well groomed hair and frequently use hairdressers.

Artesania are interesting places for tourists to visit. Centres of local handicraft such as embroidery, leatherwork and pottery. At Carrizal the El Molino Artesania, young girls are seen at work on the Calados, a fine embroidery of drawn thread. Articles are well displayed and for sale.

At Cruz de Tejeda, the highest point in Gran Canaria, donkey rides and souvenir stalls provide tourists with added interest, after they have admired and photographed the view.

Available at Maspalomas, camel rides through the sand dunes, are recommended only for those who appreciate an adventurous journey!

6   The Canary Islands and the Islanders

History of the Canary Islands

The Canary Islands were known to the Ancient World under various names; the Greeks called them 'The Isles of the Blessed' and Homer described them as the location of the 'Elysian Fields'. Later Herodotus writing in the fifth century BC, referred to them as 'The Garden of Hesperides' and the archipelago was generally known to the Romans as 'The Fortunate Islands'. Much of the early history of the Canary Islands is uncertain and is only partly explained in the myths and legends that tell of the first inhabitants' experiences.

It seems likely the Canaries were known to seafarers well before the Spanish colonised the islands in the fifteenth century. The Phoenicians are reputed to have collected 'orchilla', a purple dye, from the islands during their explorations along the coast of North West Africa; they used the dye to colour carpets and clothes. The Roman writer Pliny the Elder (AD 23 to 79), writes of an expedition sent by King Juba the Second of Mauretania (Morocco) to The Fortunate Islands about 30 BC. Pliny tells how Juba's troops found the islands deserted but with many ruins of great buildings. The soldiers saw enormous wild dogs roaming the islands, and they brought two of the animals back to the King. Afterwards the lands became known as the 'Canis Islands', *canis* being the Latin for 'dog', and in later years the 'Islands of Dogs' was corrupted to 'Canaria'. The collective name, therefore, of the Canary Islands has nothing to do with the native bird of that name but refers to these wild dogs.

When the Spaniards arrived in the fifteenth century they found a primitive race, akin to Stone Age people, occupying the islands. How they got there and their origins still remain something of a mystery. The Encyclopaedia Britannica records that the aboriginal inhabitants of the Canary Islands were called Guanches (*Guan* — person, *Chinet* — Tenerife, thus 'Man of Tenerife').

The Guanches, now extinct, appear from their skulls and bones to have resembled the Cro-Magnon race of the Quaternary age. It seems that they may have come from central and southern Europe via North Africa in some distant age. The characteristics of grey-blue eyes and blondish hair still persist in some of the present inhabitants. In the two islands of Tenerife and Gomera the Guanche type has been retained with more purity than in the others. No inscriptions have been found in these islands so it would seem that the Guanches did not know how to write. In all the islands, except these two, Semitic inscriptions and rock signs have been discovered. From these facts it would seem that people from the neighbourhood of Carthage and the Semitic races landed in the Canary Islands.

The Guanches lived in natural caves; they used to paint their bodies and wear garments of goatskin and vegetable fibres, some of which have been found in tombs in Gran Canaria. Necklaces of wood, bone and shells, polished battle axes, lances and clubs are to be seen on display in the various museums in the Canary Islands. Many cave dwellings still exist today in the mountains and remain in daily use, being handed down by each generation and much sought after as part of their heritage.

In Guanche times, many very old people, after bidding farewell to their families, were carried to a sepulchral cave, given a bowl of milk and left to die. Guanches embalmed their bodies and 'mummies' have been found wrapped in goat and sheep skins. In districts where cave dwelling was impossible they built small round houses; their communities were ruled by a king or chief.

They worshipped gods and goddesses, the sun and moon, believed in evil spirits and venerated the rocks and the mountains. Religious festivals took precedence over wars and personal quarrels.

When the Spanish conquered the islands during the fifteenth century, the Guanches are said to have put up heroic resistance against the invaders and many folk tales tell of the bravery of the doomed defenders, who in some instances preferred honourable suicide rather than ignominious defeat.

During the year 999 AD the Arabs landed and traded on Gran Canaria. In the thirteenth and fourteenth centuries Genoese, Majorcan, Portuguese and French navigators visited the islands and had a friendly welcome from the Guanches.

The eighteenth century Castillo de San José which overlooks the deep water harbour at Arrecife. Recently restored, it houses a superbly designed restaurant and modern art gallery.

Early in the fourteenth century, Lancellotto Malocello, an Italian nobleman from Genoa, discovered Lanzarote and gave his name to the island when charting a map. Although he exploited the natives for labour he made no attempt to take over the island.

The conquest of the Canary Islands by the Spanish lasted nearly a century, starting in 1402. The French nobleman, Jean de Bethancourt, under the commission of the King of Spain, together with another nobleman, Gadifer de Salle, invaded Lanzarote and Fuerteventura. After much struggle they managed to subdue the islands and to a lesser extent also La Gomera and El Hierro.

Ostensibly the Spanish invasion was to spread Christianity but they also took slaves and killed many of the inhabitants who put up a noble resistance. There was much intrigue and fighting amongst the invaders themselves when taking over the islands; this included an interim Portuguese ownership of Lanzarote and Gomera but in 1470 the Portuguese ceded their rights to the Catholic Kings' of Spain. Captain Juan Rejon was sent to claim the lands for Spain and stop fighting. In 1478 Juan Rejon landed in Gran Canaria with Castilian troops; after many cruel battles he was replaced by Pedro de Vera who in April 1483 took over the island for Spain.

Alonso de Lugo and his forces also fought many battles against the Guanches before their resistance was broken. The majority were killed in battle, some taken as slaves, a few were assimilated amongst the invaders. In 1492 La Palma fell, then in 1496 the final battle was fought at La Victoria de Acentejo in Tenerife, so at last the conquest was over and the entire archipelago was incorporated into the Crown of Castile.

When in 1492 Christopher Columbus began his search for the New World, he put into Las Palmas, Gran Canaria for repairs to his ships, later he sailed on to La Gomera for water and victuals. On future voyages he returned several times to the islands, especially La Gomera, where it is reputed he was enamoured with the beautiful widow Beatriz de Bobadilla, whom he had met previously at the Spanish court.

The Canaries became a useful staging post between Europe and the Americas, but were subject to attacks by pirates from many countries, including the English, Dutch and the Moors who were looking for slaves and timber. During the sixteenth and seventeenth centuries the islands began to prosper with the cultivation of the vine, the production of sugar, and ship repairs. Canary 'sack' or 'malmsey' wine was much sought after by Elizabethan sailors such as Raleigh and Drake.

Records show that Thomas Nichols, a 'factor' of an English company which traded in sugar, lived in Tenerife from 1556 to 1571. He wrote a book *The Fortunate Islands,* published in London in 1583.

In 1589 Philip II of Spain created the post of Captain General of the Canaries, fortifications were built as a means of defence and protection from raiding pirates and other invaders. Many of these fortresses remain to this day and form museums of interest to the tourist. So during the following years the islands developed and prospered, but a serious challenge to Spanish sovereignty was made by the British under Lord Nelson in 1797. They were repulsed in the Battle of Santa Cruz de Tenerife, where Nelson lost an arm, one hundred and twenty three British sailors were wounded and two hundred and twenty-six killed.

The Paisley and Little Company of London carried out a thriving business between 1770 and 1834. They exported Canarian wine and in return, imported to the Canaries textiles, flour, tobacco and English manufactured goods. Major business houses were established by the late eighteenth century and firms like Yeowards from Liverpool and Elders and Fyffes from London both had banana and shipping trade based on the islands.

In 1823 the Canary Islands were united to become a single province of Spain with its capital at Santa Cruz de Tenerife, this caused much annoyance to Gran Canaria, who thought that Las Palmas was of equal importance and deserved the title. The Law of Free Ports was passed in 1852, turning the archipelago into a duty free area and allowing the Canarians to trade with whole world. Although Spain remained neutral during the First World War, the drop in maritime traffic had a harmful effect on the islands.

In 1927 the archipelago was declared two provinces of Spain, each with its own capital and council.

The provinces are:-
Western Province
Tenerife (capital, Santa Cruz de Tenerife), La Gomera, El Hierro and La Palma.
Eastern Province
Gran Canaria (capital, Las Palmas), Fuerteventura, Lanzarote with the islets of Los Lobos, Graciosa, Montana Clara, Alegranza, Roque del Oeste and Roque del Este.
There is still friendly rivalry between the two provinces.

It was while serving as Military Governor of the Canary Islands that, in 1936, General Franco plotted then led the anti-Socialist revolt that sparked off the Spanish Civil War, and the Canary Islands were used as a base for training the revolutionary troops.

During the Second World War, Spain and the Canaries remained neutral. After the war, as a result of the development of modern refrigeration and commercial air transport, the agricultural industries of the islands improved. Ports were enlarged to cope with modern shipping, airports were built or enlarged.

Tourism which started with a great boom at the beginning of 1970's is now a major industry and an all-the-year-round influx of sun seeking visitors has taken people away from the land to work in hotels and shops. The Canary Islands today with a population of 1,500,000 are peaceful, progressive and working hard for a stable economy.

Canarian Way of Life

The Canarian way of life is like that in Spain — out-going and friendly. The Canarians like to sing, play music and dance whenever possible. For no reason at all they may greet you and shake hands. To pass a Canarian you know and not greet him is an insult. It is impossible to rush Canarians into taking a decision, but given time they will be pleased to help you, particularly if you are in trouble. Should you ask the way to a place, it is quite likely that you will be taken there, or someone else will be asked to assist you.

They are a proud people who dress well, with hair neatly groomed. They do not like tourists wearing scanty clothing other than on the beaches.

Although the bars and cafes are open all day and not closed until late at night, drunkenness is very rare indeed. Thankfully, there are few cripples or beggars in the streets. Disabled people are allowed to sell lottery tickets at street corners in the towns. Old people are cared for by their families.

The visitor will notice the pace of life will seem slower, people do not rush about frantically as in North European countries. The Spanish word *mañana* meaning tomorrow, often applies — why hurry?

Communal activities are ritualised. The evening gossip, called the *paseo,* is still enjoyed in every town and village, especially in the *plaza mayor* (main square). As the sun begins to set, people walk slowly up and down the streets, the air is filled with gay chatter. Children play in the plazas, young girls giggle and smile at the boys. Families sit outside cafés talking with friends while at the corners stand patient lottery ticket sellers and gipsies displaying embroidered tablecloths and souvenirs. The Guardia Civil (police) in their singular black patent-leather hats pace slowly about, always in pairs, their revolvers hanging at the ready. They, too, will stop for a coffee and a chat. Young children are allowed to stay up late so that the whole family get together in a restaurant or on a park bench. Canarians love their children very much, and are always pleased to talk about them. It is a good form of introduction if you make a pleasant remark about a child.

The islanders consider themselves to be *Canarios,* not as Spaniards, whom they talk of as *Peninsulares.* The people of Gran Canaria are also known as *Canarios,* those from Fuerteventura as *Mahohs* and Lanzarote as *Conejos.*

Although the Spanish culture naturally has predominating influence, there are also South American, Portugese and British undertones. The British community, now numbering about 6,000, has for many years contributed to the business way of life. It is only comparatively recently with the growth of tourism that German and Scandinavian entrepreneurs have infiltrated.

The cheerful Canarians realise that tourism is an economic necessity for them, and their good-natured acceptance of hordes of foreigners is to be admired.

Language

The Canarians speak Spanish. The accent and pronunciation is slightly different in each island but for Spanish speakers there is not much problem with comprehension. Canarians generally make an effort to communicate, and many also speak English, German and French.

Nowadays English is taught as a second language in the higher grade schools. So if you have a query you are more likely to get an answer from a student than from an older person. In the smaller country villages it may be hard to find someone who understands English at all. Thus it is sensible to carry an English/Spanish dictionary and phrase book, also a local map, when seeking directions and information. (See also Appendix 'B'.)

Flora and fauna

A botanist's paradise

The Canary Islands have been called a botanist's paradise: the physical characteristics of the islands and their climate with little variation between the seasons combine to produce a diversity of environments for a variety of flora, within a relatively small area. The islands are a true Garden of Eden where dark, dense forests give way to heathers, gorses and bracken. Steep green valley are terraced with eucalyptus, mimosa, cork trees and broom. Lush meadows harbour butterflies, dragonflies and ladybirds amongst the wild marigolds and buttercups. Oases of palm trees give shade for the cultivation of alfalfa, while cineraria and honeysuckle mingle in the hedgerows.

In the populated areas of the island, in parks and gardens, geraniums, rosy hibiscus, carnations, marigolds, nasturtiums and bougainvillea bring a riot of colour, sometimes growing wild along the verges. The poinsettia, often in double form and of various hues from deep red to pale lemon, grows into thick hedges as high as trees. The exotic strelitzia, the bird of paradise flower with its waxen blue, white and orange blossom, and birdlike shape, has now become established as the Canary Islands symbolic flower. And one of the greatest delights of the islands is the sweet perfume of their wild aromatic plants and exotic flowers. Laburnums, honeysuckle, broom, eucalyptus, pine, many more, blend together to create a wonderful nosegay from nature.

About 1,800 different species of plants grow wild. Some have been here since the late Tertiary period: fossilised plants have been discovered, similar to those found in Mediterranean areas dating from that time. One of the last surviving trees of the Tertiary era, is the Dracaena draco, which may be called a living fossil. The tree is known as the dragon tree, or dragon's blood tree, because of the resinous secretions which, when exposed to the air, turn a dark, blood red. The one at **Icod de los Vinos** in Tenerife is reputed to be at least 3,000 years old. It is a weird sight, with its main thick trunk branching out into many more trunks, and a massive ridged top with spiky green leaves. The Guanches attributed magical powers to the sap of the dragon tree and thought it a cure for various ailments.

Seen in the arid areas of south Gran Canaria, the Cardon Cactus, which looks like candelabra, has sharp spikes that ooze sticky sap when broken.

Botanical Gardens and National Parks

Each wave of newcomers has introduced new varieties of plants to the Canaries, and since the Middle Ages the islands have been used for acclimatising tropical plant species before taking them to colder climates. The Botanical Gardens in Tenerife and Gran Canaria contain thousands of rare exotic plants and botanical gems from all over the world, as well as endemic species, and these gardens are well worth a visit.

There is much to be seen, also, in the National Parks.

In the **Teide National Park** (Tenerife) there grows a small violet (*viola cheiranthifolio*) adapted to the strong sun and dry conditions — the only living plant found 3,000 m above sea level. Another plant growing in this area is the red Tajinaste or Teide Vipers Bugloss (Pride of Tenerife). It is one of the most admired plants in the park: with its single stem growing up to two metres high, it is densely covered with reddish blossoms and makes a striking picture against the dry volcanic soil. Other species include the laburnum with its bright yellow flowers and the Teide Broom or Broom of the Peak (*Retama del Pico*). At the end of April a profusion of highly fragrant pink and white blossoms sprout from its stiff twigs, presenting a unique sight for, in the whole world, it is only in the stony and lofty regions of the Tiede National Park and La Palma that this plant survives.

Caldera de Taburiente National Park (La Palma) is very different from the Teide National Park because of the abundance of water in the region; numerous fountains spring from the earth becoming streams and waterfalls. The landscape of the park is shaped by the Canary pine *(pinus Canariensis*). This species constitutes nature's important defence against erosion. Others growing in profusion are the *Faya* or *La Haya,* an arborescent shrub which has oblong and pointed leaves related to the tree heath, small hollies like *ilex platyphylla* and the big *Barbusano* trees.

Timanfaya National Park, in the western part of Lanzarote, is an area of intensive volcanic eruptions dominated by inorganic or mineral components. The lower part of the park is an immense field of solidified lava where vegetal species are only just beginning to colonise the arid ground. Aeonios or semperuivums, and tabaibas, the sturdy euphorbias, can be seen clinging to the bare rocks. These desert plants make welcome patches of green, but Lanzarote's National Park is not the place to go to study flora or fauna!

Banana plantations abound in the Canary Islands. Some are protected behind high walls, but others are open for tourists to see those green fingers that seem to grow up side down!

101

Garajonay National Park (Gomera), situated in the centre of the island, is a mixture of crags, hills, slopes and gorges. More than half the area is covered with Laurisilva forest (Laurisilva is a sub tropical formation dating from the Tertiary era); the principal trees that make up the Laurisilva are the laurel, the linden, heather and the small holly. A characteristic of the forest of Garajonay is that trees have trunks and branches which are covered with age-old lichen and moss. Hanging down in fairy like gossamer, it gives an eerie and bewitched air of mystery.

Apart from the National Parks, the islands have numerous places where wild flowers, ferns and trees grow in great profusion. In many ways it is unfortunate that the majority of popular tourist resorts are situated in the drier and more desert-like areas. With such a variety of entertainment and golden beaches nearby, some visitors never find the time to visit the less populated, verdant areas, and they come away with a one-sided impression of the beauty of the Canary Islands.

Wildlife

The islands' fauna are less numerous than the plants, the most famous being the giant lizards of El Hierro (*lacerta simonyi*) which grow to a length of 1 metre. Recently thought to be extinct they have again been discovered, but their whereabouts is a guarded secret. Smaller versions of these lizards, the Tizon, can sometimes be observed in the drier regions; they are quite harmless. There are no poisonous snakes and only a few scorpions, mosquitoes and flies. Rabbits, hares, goats, camels, donkeys and similar animals have been introduced by man.

Bird life is varied. There are over two hundred species, some so well adapted to life on the islands that they can fly only short distances. There are many pigeons, partridge, quail, blackbirds, robins and sparrows. Birds of prey such as crows, vultures, buzzards, white eagles and sparrow hawks are seen frequently. Perhaps disappointingly the native Canary bird (*sarinus Canaria*) which is completely yellow when domesticated, is a brownish colour with only touches of yellow in the wild; but its song is still sweet. The Tenerife chaffinch has an iridescent black and blue plumage. But perhaps the most striking bird seen is the hoopoe, whose bold black and white wing pattern, erectile crest, pink-brown plumage and long curved bill, make it instantly recognisable; its 'hoo poo poo' call carries far.

The melody of the bird song can be heard in many parks and gardens all over the islands. The National Parks, too, provide ornithologists with much to observe and note.

Migrant birds use the Canary Islands, especially seabirds crossing the Atlantic. Birds from North Africa, too, visit Fuerteventura and the sandy Jandia beaches: little egrets, sandpipers and curlews search the inland saltwater pools for food.

Brilliant butterflies, dragonflies, moths and other small insects breed in the green vegetal areas of the Canaries. The cochineal insect (*coccus cacti*) is bred on the Nopal, a prickly pear type cactus, mainly in Lanzarote; it is used to make the cochineal dye which gives a red colouring to edibles like sweets, toothpaste and lipstick. Transparent-winged cicadas with their shrill chirping, fill the air with the sounds of a tropical night.

Agriculture

Two important factors influencing climate and, consequently agriculture in the Canaries are the winds, which blow in from the Atlantic and the north-east (trade winds), and the Gulf Stream, which flows in to warm the colder Canaries currents. The winds bring clouds which, when they hit the high mountainous areas, condense to give rain. Thus, in those islands which have a central mountainous zone, we find that the northern and western parts are humid and verdant, while the southern parts, beyond the mountains, are drier and less fertile. Much less rain falls on the islands of Lanzarote and Fuerteventura because these are much flatter; besides they are nearer to the coast of Africa and are subject to hot winds blowing from the Sahara.

At one time the economy of the islands rested on the cultivation of sugar cane, but it became unprofitable; then the vine took over — Canary sack and Malvasia were as popular as Madeira — but this too failed. Sugar and wine are still produced but today the main crop is bananas. These are exported all over the world but for economic reasons the main market is Spain. Tomatoes, potatoes and cucumbers are also important exports, and various other vegetables — such as peppers, aubergines and onions — are produced for overseas markets. In recent years the export of flowers, by air, has increased: these are mainly roses, carnations and the islands' brilliant strelitzias. Cereals, salads, greens, beans, apples and pears are cultivated mostly for the local market.

Tobacco is grown, mainly in La Palma, where factories produce cigars which have a high reputation. The cigarette industry is important in both Tenerife and Gran Canaria.

The little Canary banana, *musa cavendishii,* is deliciously sweet, to be enjoyed when there. Sometimes, as with the tomato, it is difficult to purchase the ripe fruit because they are cropped when very green. One frequently encounters huge lorries carrying enormous loads of the heavy 'hands' of green bananas along narrow country roads; they can make travelling very slow.

On all the islands the country people work long and hard, often with hand tools, sometimes assisted by donkeys and camels — an incongruous sight. Modern machinery is gradually being introduced both in the field and packing shed.

A special mention must be made of the great endeavour with which the people of Lanzarote and Fuerteventura cultivate their lands. The persistance of the peasants to produce their crops despite severe water shortages and volcanic soil arouses admiration.

Their ingenious method of creating moisture in the land is to dig deep saucers, filling them with volcanic ash, so retaining moisture from the early morning dew to stop the roots from drying out. Sometimes the crops have to be protected from strong winds by windbreaks made from lava stones and grasses. Even so in a dry winter whole fields of crops may wither and die without sufficient moisture. So if you should be on the islands on one of the rare rainy days do not complain too much; rain is so precious and much prayed for by all the Canarians.

Fishing Industry

Fish is part of the staple diet of the islanders particularly those who live by the sea. They will often use a boat for inshore fishing during the night. In the early morning the entire family will be on the beach to help pull in the boats and assist with the catch. You can help too!

Many Canarians are involved with sea fishing. the main catches being tuna, swordfish, mackerel and sardine, all of which are used for export and canning. The seas around are full of fish, great shoals are found in the waters that lie between Lanzarote, Fuerteventura and North Africa; but unfortunately the fishing fleets are poorly equipped.

Sport fishing is popular in these waters and many world record catches have been made, especially from Puerto Rico, Gran Canaria.

National Holidays

Shops and offices are closed on the following national feast or *fiesta* days. Bars, restaurants, theatres and cinemas are open, however, and public transport operates though sometimes the services are limited (as on Sundays).

January	1	— New Year's Day
January	6	— Epiphany
March	19	— San José
(variable)		— Good Friday
		— Easter Monday
May	1	— Labour Day
(variable		— Corpus Christi
(variable)		— Ascension
June	29	— San Pedro and San Pablo
July	18	— National Day
July	25	— Santiago Apostal
August	15	— The Assumption
October	12	— Día de la Hispanidad
November	1	— All Saints
December	8	— Immaculate Concepción
December	25	— Christmas Day

In addition each city, town and village holds religious festivals and *fiestas* for its own patron saints. Christmas (*Navidad*) is celebrated with shops being decorated and there are scenes of the Nativity and the Three Wise Kings, for it is mainly a religious festival.

December 31st (*Noche Vieja*) is much enjoyed with parties, bonfires and fireworks. At midnight the New Year is heralded with the eating of twelve grapes, one at each strike of the clock, amidst great merriment and hooting of car horns and ships' sirens.

January 6th is the day for religious services, then the giving of presents — the most exciting day of the year for all children. Families dress in their best clothes and parade the streets and plazas, with the children showing off their new toys.

Fiestas and Festivals

These are taken very seriously in the Canary Islands; religious services and processions are full of fervour. Visitors are always allowed to join in the processions and are made welcome if due respect is observed.

Once the religious part of the day is accomplished the fun and games start. Sport is part of the Canary way of life at all ages, and singing and dancing come naturally even wee toddlers are encouraged to join in, whatever the hour. Folklore too is part of every fiesta and some interesting customs are still observed. For instance at the festival of **Bajada del Cristo** in Telde, Gran Canaria, an unusual statue of Christ is paraded through the streets of the town. Brought back by returning conquistadores, it was made by the Mexican Indians from maize, mixed with water into a kind of papier maché, and is still much revered.

Tourist fiestas are full of fun with beauty queens, decorated floats, many bands, drum majorettes and clowns. The larger fiestas in Las Palmas (Gran Canaria), Santa Cruz de Tenerife and La Palma are more like the carnivals of South America with elaborate costumes and masks, and fireworks and dancing continuing all night. The streets can be very crowded in the larger towns where care should be taken against pickpockets.

The Floral Carpets created to celebrate Corpus Christi (May/-June), are a tremendous feat of endeavour, a true works of art. These are said to have started in La Orotava, when an aristocratic lady laid some flowers on the cobbled street outside her house before a religious procession. People copied her, so evolved the carpets of flowers. Now intricate religious scenes and colourful floral patterns are created, using chalk patterns or metal frames which are later removed. Coloured volcanic sands, pebbles, salt and grains of cereal are used in some villages, while others only use leaves and flowers. After the religious procession has trodden over the carpets a battle of flowers creates much gaiety. You can see Floral Carpets at La Laguna in Tenerife and Las Palmas, Gran Canaria.

At Tacoronte in the north of Tenerife, the Fiestas del Cristo last for two weeks from 7—12 September. The principal events are held on the two Saturdays and Sundays with solemn Masses and street processions. There are also livestock shows, cycle races, sporting events, a car rally and Canarian wrestling (*lucha*). Dances and balls take place most evenings with folklore and classical concerts. As well, it is a time for lots of drinking for this is the time of the grape harvest, and Tacoronte is in the heart of Tenerife's best red wine producing country. Tourists are welcome to join in all the celebrations.

It is worth noting that overnight accommodation is particularly hard to find at fiesta time, so do book in advance.

Calendar of fiestas and festivals
Gran Canaria

January 5 Cabalgata de los Reyes Magos (Las Palmas, Teror, Aguimes and Galdar)

January 20 Festival of Almond Blossom Tejeda and Valseequillo)

February Carnival (Las Palmas, Telde and Aguimes)

February Fiestas Turisticas de Invierno (San Augustin, Maspalomas and Playa del Inglés) specially for tourists.

March/April Semana Santa (Holy Week), (all island especially Las Palmas and Telde)

April 29 Festival to commemorate the incorporation of the island with the Crown of Castile (Las Palmas).

May Fiesta de San Isidro (Galdar, Teror, San Nicholas de Tolentino and Montano Cardones)

May/June Corpus Christi (flower carpets) (Las Palmas and Arucas).

June 24 Fiesta to celebrate the foundation of Las Palmas (Las Palmas, Telde and Arucas)

July 6 Fiesta de San Isidro (Teror)

July 6 Fiesta del Albaricoque (apricots) (Fataga)

July 16 Fiesta del Carmen (Las Palmas Galdar, San Nicholas de Tolentine).

July 25 Feast of Saint James the Apostle (San Bartolome de Tirajana and Galdar).

August 4 La Bajada de la Rama (Agaete) of special tourist interest.

August 15 Fiesta de San Roque (Guia, Telde and Las Palmas)

August last Sunday Fiesta de la Virgen de la Cuevita (Artenara)

September 8 Fiesta de la Virgen del Pino (all island).

September 10 Fiesta de San Nicholas (San Nicholas de Tolentino).

September 10 Bajado del Cristo (Telde)

October first Sunday Fiesta de la Naval (Las Palmas and Santa Bridgida), celebrating the victory over Sir Francis Drake.

November Rancho de Animas (folk music and dancing) (Teror)

December 8 Fiesta de la Cana Dulce (Arucas and Santa Lucia).

December 25 Navidades (all island)

December 31 Nochevieja (all island) firework display.

Fuerteventura

February 2 Celebrations to honour the Virgin of Candelaria (La Oliva)

July 14 Fiesta del Patron San Buenaventura (Betancuria).

July 16 Fiesta de la Virgen del Carmen (Corralejo)

September Third Saturday Fiesta de la Virgen de la Pena, (Betancuria).

October 1 - 6 Fiesta de la Virgen Rosario (Puerto del Rosario)

October 10 - 13 Fiesta de San Miguel (Gran Tarajal)

Lanzarote

January 5 Cabalgata de los Reyes Magos (Teguise)

February Carnival (Arrecife)

June 24 Fiesta de San Juan (Haria)

June 29 Fiesta de San Pedro (Maguez)

July 7 Fiesta de San Marcial del Rubicon (Playa Blanco Sur)

July 16 Fiesta de la Nuestra Señora del Carmen (Teguise)

August all the month Fiesta de San Gines (all island). Traditional dancing, camel drawn carts.

September 8 Fiesta de Nuestra Señora Guadalupe (Teguise)

September 15 Fiesta de Virgen de los Volcanes (Tinajo).

Canary Music and Dancing

The Canarians are a musical people, who love to sing and dance on every occasion. From a very early age toddlers are encouraged to make music; visitors to the islands are charmed to see tiny children who clap their hands and sing to a natural rhythm while at play.

Each island has its own folk dances and songs, but the general influence is Spanish and South American. The flute and tambourine are popular but the islands' most typical instrument is the *timple*. Much like a small guitar or ukelele, the *timple* was first made at Teguise in Lanzarote where there are still craftsmen making this delightful instrument.

Canary folk song and dances have a typical swaying movement, with languid drawn out melodies; gestures and brightly coloured costumes combine to make a unique and exotic impression. The *folia* is slow, the man demonstrating his feelings for the woman with dignity and restraint. *Folia* songs have been compared with the Portuguese *fado*. The *isa* is a light and gay dance similar to an English country dance.

The costumes worn by men and women are highly decorative. The women wear brightly coloured, often striped, skirts over long white petticoats; sometimes the overskirts are delicately embroidered and looped up. Dainty lace-trimmed aprons and embroidered waistcoats fit neatly over white blouses with large puff sleeves. Black ankle boots, scarves and hats complete the picture. It is the type of hat which helps to identify the islander: in the eastern islands, the scarf covers the face more and the hat is wider brimmed. In Tenerife and La Palma the hat is tilted towards the back of the head.

The men's costumes include white shirts, black knee length trousers over white underbreeches, long red waistcoats and colourful cummerbunds or sashes. Woollen knee-length socks and white spats over black shoes are worn and a soft black felt hat. Sometimes a thick cape completes the costume.

Students from various Spanish universities can frequently be seen in carnival costume, singing and playing in bars, restaurants and plazas to collect money for charity.

At fiesta time glittering masks are sold, and everyone delights in dressing up. Young girls paint their faces and nails, flashing smiles in all directions and young men wear flowing capes and carry guitars.

Exhibitions and galas of Canarian music and folk dancing are held regularly on all the islands, throughout the year. Some are planned for the tourist, but most are for the delight of the happy Canarians, whose greatest pleasure is to make music and dance.

Folklore

Canary folklore thrives with the different islands keeping to their own traditions. This is very noticable in the varying styles of dress, singing and dancing. Religious fiestas often begin with a *Romeria* (pilgrimage), a long procession of people with gaily decorated horses and carts; in Lanzarote camel drawn carts are used.

Special programmes for each town are preserved and presented each year. Acrobats, clowns and dwarfs perform in the street, great battles are re-enacted with much vigour. In Santa Cruz de la Palma the Fiesta of the Descent of the Virgin, has taken place uninterruptedly for three hundred years.

Handicrafts

All the islands retain many craftsmen and women, in some instances their skills are unique. Craftsmanship has played an important part in architecture as can be seen in the old Canary houses and churches. Implements like yokes and ploughs, kitchen utensils, beautiful looms for weaving, furniture, cedar chests and pipes for smoking, all have over the years been carefully carved from the many different types of wood growing locally. Musical instruments, too, like the Canarian guitar (*timple*) and castanets (*chacaras*) are still being made by traditional methods. The typical Canary **basketwork** had its origin in its use for agriculture.

Vara (twig) basketwork is very sturdy; made from strips of young wood like chestnut, in La Palma it reaches an outstanding quality, whilst in Tenerife it is executed with darker, wider and thicker strips of wood.

Cana (cane) basketwork can be pure cane for making delicate baskets, or a mixture of cane and twig for strength. *Palanqueta* where strips are obtained from the stalks of bunches of dates, gives a highly decorative effect. Very sturdy baskets are made on the island of Hierro, especially at Sardinero.

Other basketwork produces hats, mats and handbags made from the palm leaf. The central stem of the palm, the *pirgano* can be used for fans and brooms. In Ingenio, Gran Canaria another strong strong basket is made from reeds. Straw can be used on its own or tied with bramble, to make hampers and containers for dried fruit. Each island keeps to its own traditional work.

110

Calados is the drawn threadwork embroidery that is made in many Canarian homes. At Lajares demonstrations of the work are given to admiring tourists.

There is renewed interest amongst the young in the ancient arts, especially amongst potters who work alongside the old crafts people. The main characteristic of typical Canary **pottery** is its simplicity and non use of the wheel, the craftsmans hands being the only means of lifting and rotating the clay. A small amount of sand is put under the clay to stop it adhering to the ground or bench.

It is fascinating to watch the work of someone like Dona Guadalupe Nubla, in the village of Chipude tucked away in the craggy mountains of Gomera. The shapes of the pots remain the same as in Guanche times.

The pottery being produced in Lanzarote is yet another form of art, as created by Juan Brito, who's style is more abstract. In La Palma, the Benahorita people (the ancient inhabitants) bequeathed a unique type of pottery which has a wonderful glaze, and is marked with prehistoric spirals and geometrical designs. It can be purchased at Mazo and in Santa Cruz de la Palma.

Weaving is still worked on handlooms. Traditional *traperas* rugs, made from rags, are sometimes now woven with wool. Always in bright colours, they make lovely souvenir presents. Among the places where you can see this work done is the *artesania* (craftshop) near Hermigua in Gomera. At El Paso in La Palma you can find a unique example of silk weaving.

It is also in La Palma that wonderful silk shawls are delicately **hand embroidered.** The *bordados* tablecloths of La Palma are of such a high standard of craft that they are considered amongst the finest work of the islands. Although expensive to purchase they make magnificent heirlooms.

The handicraft that tourists can most easily observe and purchase is **open threadwork** (*calcados*). The work is done mainly in Tenerife, Gran Canaria and Fuerteventura, but it is a cottage industry pursued when conditions do not allow work in the fields. *Calados* is executed by stretching the cloth on a frame, and drawing the threads together to form an intricate pattern. Usually each piece is worked by more than one person. Each island has its own designs and it is interesting to compare these. The same patterns appear on the blouses and skirts worn by the folk dancers.

Various schools of needlework throughout the islands are now open to visitors and the articles sold there are usually a little less expensive than in the shops. Seeing pretty young twelve-year-olds patiently working their needle must surely make you reach for your purse to keep alive the art of hand embroidery.

It is impossible to write about the preservation of handicrafts and traditions in the Canaries, without mentioning the work of Cesar Manrique. Born in Lanzarote, he is an artist and sculptor of international renown. Lanzarote has become an ecological focus point for the way he has protected the environment and harmonised new developments with the landscape. No more high rise apartments, bill posters, advertisement boardings or rubbish in Lanzarote: it has to be seen to be believed. It was he who designed the superb Lago Martinez of which the people of Tenerife are justly proud.

The list of handicrafts of the islands is long, and one must mention a few more, delicate lace work done by the convent sisters, rag dolls dressed in typical costume, woollen shawls, native clay figures, polished volcanic stones. (the *peridot* is a green semi precious stone which is made into attractive jewellery).

Thanks to the patience of the islanders and the support of many tourists, the folklore and crafts are being preserved.

There are many windmills on Fuerteventura, most of which are still in daily use for drawing water or grinding corn.

7 Gran Canaria
Isla de Contraste — Island of Contrasts

The island of Gran Canaria, Island of Contrasts, is the third largest of the Canary Islands with a population of some 550,000 and a surface area of 1532 sq km. In shape it resembles a giant pyramid, the central high mountains of Cruz de Tejeda culminating in the peak of El Pozo de las Nieves (the well of snow), 1932m. Often referred to as a 'continent in miniature', the island of Gran Canaria offers an enormous variety of landscapes; scenery varies from high mountains with rugged peaks to large stretches of golden sands, and deep ravines (*barrancos*) divide the land, stretching inland from the coast. The north is green and cultivated but in the hot dry south only goats graze and cacti grow.

The capital of Gran Canaria, **Las Palmas,** is the largest urban centre in the Canary archipelago. It is from Las Palmas that the government administers the islands of Fuerteventura and Lanzarote. Las Palmas is also an international port, the most important in Spain, so it is constantly busy with cruise liners, tankers, cargo and fishing boats. It is a 'duty-free' port — an added attraction for tourists.

Las Palmas is situated in the north-east corner of the island. Attached to it by a narrow strip of land is a tiny peninsula, **La Isleta,** now a military base and closed to the public. There are two fine sandy beaches, Playa de las Canteras on the north coastline and Playa de Alcaravaneras on the east coastline, south of the port. Hotels of international status mingle with shops large and small, with churches, monuments, parks and gardens, in this colourful, noisy city, full of life and activity.

114

Since it is within easy reach of Europe, Africa and the Americas, a constant flow of visitors arrive by sea and air. A regular passenger/car ferry service operating from Cadiz (Southern Spain) to Las Palmas makes the sea crossing in 48 hours. At the Aeropuerto de Gando, on the east coast 19 km from Las Palmas, jet airliners arrive frequently from London (flight time 5 hours), Madrid (less than two hours), New York (seven hours) and all over the world.

Most of the holiday hotel and villa complexes are located in the south of the island where the climate is drier. At resorts like San Agustin, Playa del Inglés and Puerto Rico, vast blocks of apartments and hotels cater for the visitors. The combination of sunshine, sea and extensive golden sands, provides endless pleasure and entertainment. With its spring-like climate, Gran Canaria is invigorating, giving a feeling of well-being. No need for overcoats in Gran Canaria; even on the few days when rain falls or the *sirocco* (a hot dusty wind from North Africa) blows only a lightweight windproof coat is required.

Away from the bright lights of the coastal resorts, small fishing villages provide a quieter way of life. Arguineguin and Puerto de las Nieves are two places where fish are of prime importance and you can discover little fish restaurants with an informal atmosphere. Inland towns are full of character, narrow streets have attractive typically Canarian, wooden balconies. Churches are set in cool, tree-lined squares. At Arucas the large Gothic-style church rises majestically above the town, surrounded by huge banana plantations, a sea of waving green leaves.

A visit must be made to the volcanic crater of La Caldera de Bandama, now covered in vegetation. From the *mirador* (viewpoint) above, there is a splendid panoramic view over the island and out to the blue Atlantic.

Perfect peace can be found in the dense forests of Pinar de Tamadaba, where the sweet smell of pines fills the air. Drive up the valley of Los Berrazales, a paradise of colour, where bougainvillea mingles with bright poinsettia growing way above the height of man. Tall palms, papaya and avocado trees and coffee create a landscape of beauty; terraced fields yield plentiful crops of potatoes, tomatoes, sweet corn and aubergines. You can hear the distant sound of bells from the goats as they climb high into the mountains. Nearby caves now updated with television aerials are still being used as dwellings by Canarians.

Climate

Gran Canaria has an agreeable climate varying between 17.8 degrees C in winter and 24 degrees C in midsummer. The rainfall is light — only about fifty days in the year and often only a short shower, — mainly in the high central mountains and the north of the island. Indeed in the extreme south at Puerto Rico rainfall is light, only about fifty days in the year and often only a short shower, mainly in the high central mountains and the Humidity at sea level, especially in Las Palmas, can be as high as 70 per cent. Light breezes with clear blue skies and brilliant sunshine are the main features of the weather. Winds are predominantly northwesterly occasionally veering to easterly, when they bring hot air and dust from North Africa. The sea temperature is always 19-20 degrees C.

Clothes

Swimwear, of course, and lightweight cotton and drip-dry clothes are the main requirements; for touring the mountains, a thin wool cardigan or windproof jacket is advisable. It is not favourably received if you wear scanty clothing away from the beach or promenade. Use of a sun hat, sunglasses and suntan cream are recommended, as the rays of the sun are 15 per cent stronger here than in Europe.

Getting about

Travel around the island offers little problem. Car hire firms are to be found in all major tourist areas and at the airport. A regular bus service runs between the larger towns, though less frequently to the smaller villages. Road surfaces round the coast are good, with a fast motorway from the airport to Las Palmas. Inland the roads can be tortuous, with unguarded edges; practically all give scenic drives, but you must drive with caution.

History

Gran Canaria still has visible links with its ancient history: the vast number of old caves and artefacts help us to build up a picture of the original primitive inhabitants, the Guanches, who must have lived here peacefully enough, warding of incursions by slaves and adventurers, until the fifteenth century.

The greatest change in the history of the island came in 1478, when Juan Rejon was charged by the Spanish Catholic king to convert the natives to Christianity.

It is said that Rejon and his soldiers landed on the tiny islet, La Isleta, at the northeast tip of Gran Canaria. Using local palms they built themselves a protective palisade around their camp, calling it Real de las Palmas (camp of the palms), later the name was simplified to Las Palmas.

After long years of bitter fighting and heroic resistance, the island chief Doramas, died in a bloody battle at Arucas.

But it was not finally conquered until 1483, and it took until 1487 for it to be incorporated into the Spanish Crown. Las Palmas became the seat of the archipelagos bishopric and the building of the Cathedral of Santa Ana was begun.

Christopher Columbus took advantage of the port on his way up to the New World. The island's carpenters and craftsmen were able to do useful repairs to his ships; water and provisions were taken aboard.

Sugar canes were imported from Madeira together with vines, and these grew well in the fertile soil. Merchants and traders set up business in the thriving port. In 1515 a Military Governor was appointed to build defensive fortifications against attacking pirates.

With the increase of trade between America and Europe, the importance of Las Palmas as a port of call became even greater. In 1778 laws promulgated freedom of trade between the Indies and the Canaries, and Las Palmas enjoyed much prosperity; and in 1852 the Law of Free Ports was passed which turned the whole archipelago into a duty free area, allowing the Canarians to trade with the whole world.

Today Las Palmas is the archipelago's industrial centre, with oil refinery, chemical, textile and tobacco factories.

Gran Canaria has the largest livestock population of all the islands, cattle, sheep, pigs and goats contribute to the economy. Enough bananas, tomatoes and cucumbers are produced for export despite the great shortage of water for cultivation.

However, in the last ten years the tourist industry has developed rapidly and is now a major economic factor, and still on the increase.

Las Palmas, the capital

For some the name Las Palmas evokes pictures of cruise liners and tropical islands, but in fact Las Palmas is not in the tropics, and its climate is not always as perfect as many expect. Often clouds descend from the mountains to mix with the warm air currents and create a humidity that can be oppressive. Nevertheless thousands of tourists from all over the world pour into the city.

The combination of busy port with ancient and modern city makes Las Palmas a centre of international importance. Huge docks and harbour walls protect the shipping in the Puerto de la Luz, day and night there is activity among cargo and passenger ships. Fishing boats, too, jostle for a berth alongside the quays. The jetfoil from Tenerife and ships of the Trasmediterranea Company draw up alongside the Muelle Santa Catalina, from where it is but a short distance to the centre of the city. A newly erected terminal building has a booking office, parking and clean toilets. Taxis meet all ships. Those arriving by sea have a good view of the wide expanse of the city which has developed behind the bustling port — the round tower of the modern Hotel Los Bardineros making a distinctive landmark.

The port and its environs

The Castillo de la Luz is one of the outstanding features of the port area. It is the oldest historic monument in Las Palmas, originally a fortress built in 1494 and recently restored.

As one leaves the Muelle Santa Catalina, still inside the dock area, there is a shop called Sovhispan, mainly for the benefit of visiting Russian sailors, selling a variety of Russian goods including genuine Russian vodka.

Outside the main docks area a short distance to the south is the Naval Dock, with its impressive walled entrance always heavily guarded. Opposite the Muelle, across the traffic lights, is the Parque Santa Catalina, the hub of the modern city. This is not so much a park as a plaza, with tables and chairs set out on the wide pavements. Always thronging with life, night and day, it is a great meeting place for people from all over the world. Open air cafes, stalls and bazaars welcome the tourists. Goods from Africa, the Orient, Spain, China and the Americas can be found in a wonderful, colourful jumble. Portrait painters, shoe shiners, fruitsellers, entertainers and chess players are just some of the features of this ever moving scene. Beware if you are offered a 'gold' watch, and if you are tempted to buy an embroidered tablecloth from a pretty girl you should finally expect to pay only about half the asking price. This is a splendid place to sit in the sun with your coffee, beer or brandy just watching the world go by. Try to see it at night under a moonlit starry sky, when the warm air is full of different aromas, tall waving palms and coloured lights make a brilliant background to the animated, cosmopolitan scene.

The Tourist Office is situated in the Parque Santa Catalina, easily identified by its attractive, low Canarian style building with dark wooden balcony. Inside you will find an attentive staff, presided over by the charming Senōr Arturo Tavio, who comes from an old Canarian family. He speaks excellent English and his courteous manner and affection for the islands make a visit to the Tourist Office a real pleasure. He can provide a list of accommodation in all price ranges, a map of the city and details of bus services. The office is open from 0900 to 1330 hrs and from 1700 to 1900 hrs. Saturday from 0900 to 1330 hrs, closed on Sundays and public holidays.

A shopping expedition

Shopping is delightfully easy in Gran Canaria. Las Palmas, one of the largest duty free ports in the world can provide almost every need — but do not expect everything to be exceptionally cheap — prices are generally levelling off all over Europe, and in the Canaries too. Shops are open from 0900 to 1300 hrs and 1600 to 2000 hrs, closed on Sundays and public holidays. The greatest reduction are to be found in the prices of cigarettes, alcohol, radios, watches, perfumes and electrical goods. Some shops have fixed prices, particularly those run by Canarians; in others you are expected to barter — Indian and African salesmen expect this — which is a slow method of shopping, reducing the price by mutual consent.

Supermarkets are everywhere in Gran Canaria even the smallest village will have a shop where foods on the shelves are priced and baskets and trolleys are available. Generally speaking, most shopkeepers understand English and will be helpful, often going out of their way to assist you.

The best souvenirs typical of the island are the hand-embroidered tablecloths made in a drawn-thread work called *calados*. In these days of machine-made goods opportunities to obtain such work are rare. Costume dolls, wooden ornaments and shawls are attractive buys. Gold, silver, ivory carvings, jade, fine furs and silks are moderately priced. Goods imported from Spain tend to be a little more expensive due to transport costs. Fresh fruit and vegetables are on sale in open air markets, usually once a week. In Las Palmas a covered market,

119

open from Monday to Saturday, is to be found in the old part of the town, the Vegueta.

The two major department stores of Las Palmas, El Cortes del Inglés and Galerias Preciados, can be found, on opposite sides of the road, along Avenida de José Mesa y Lopez north of the Alcaravaneras beach. Similar in layout, they are splendidly modern with six floors plus basement, and complete with escalators. Services offered are interpreters, currency exchange, cafeteria, restaurant, gift shop, home delivery and undercover parking. American Express Access and Eurocards are accepted. The basement of El Cortes del Inglés houses a large supermarket selling fresh bread, cakes, meat and vegetables. Almost next door to this store is a small branch of Marks and Spencer. However, the main shopping area of Las Palmas is around the Calle Mayor de Triana (see Triana and the Parque Doramas). It is worth going to the streets where the Canarians themselves do their shopping, away from the tourist areas, as prices are sometimes more moderate. Prices in the south of the island are generally higher than in Las Palmas.

It may be of interest to you that in Las Palmas you can have a suit made in less than one week and new spectacles can be ready in forty-eight hours!

The beaches

From the Parque Santa Catalina it is a comfortable ten-minute walk due north, along the Calle de Luis Morote to the Playa de las Canteras. On the way you will pass a conglomeration of shops all selling an array of duty free goods. The Canteras beach is rated among the world's top ten beaches — so the local people will tell you with pride! It's two and a half kilometres of golden sand can be enjoyed all the year round. Protected by **La Barra,** a natural barrier of rocks out at sea, the waters are usually calm, warm and safe for bathing. At night the long, tiled promenade is a blaze of colourful lights which reflects on the waters. The evening *paseo* (walk about) takes place here, enjoyed by local Canarians as well as holidaymakers, for the Canteras beach is close both to the centre of Las Palmas and the port — the distance between the west and east coasts is only 300 m at its narrowest part.

Las Palmas has a second big beach, not quite as long as Canteras, on the east coast running south of the port. The **Playa de las Alcaravaneras** is much used by the Canarians themselves and the waters are kept clean by an ingenious method of stringing a line of cork logs across the sea, so keeping the debris away from the beach.

Eating places

In Las Palmas you will find a wide range of eating places from simple Canarian bars to the grill room of a 5-star hotel. Self-service restaurants are of a high standard. On your return from Cantaras beach, for instance, you may wish to stop for a meal. Halfway along Calle Luis Morote turn left into Calle Tomás Millar and at no.67 you will see a large sign 'International Self Service'. The upstairs restaurant here provides a real feast of food. For the price of 425 pesetas (£2.19) per person you may choose from at least thirty-five different dishes, eating as much as you please. Laid out attractively, the food is well cooked and good value. Drinks are extra and reasonably priced: half a litre of wine 230 pesetas (£1.18), whisky 140 pesetas (72p), beers and minerals 75 pesetas (38p). There is often a Canarian folk group playing here making a collection for charity. Open 1200 to 2300 hrs. Similar self-service restaurants are to be found in the vicinity.

You will find restaurants catering for all nationalities and tastes: Chinese, South American, Indian, Japanese, Russian, German, Dutch, French, Belgian, Swiss and Scandinavian, not forgetting English and American Steakhouses. Most establishments display the menu and prices outside, in several languages. One good way to select your restaurant is to buy the local paper *Canarias Tourist,* issued monthly, 150 pesetas (77p). Written in four languages, including English, it is full of tips and information, and has an extensive list of restaurants with addresses, telephone numbers and type of food served.

Transport and excursions

Should you feel tired after shopping, use one of the many taxis that park outside the stores. In the city, metered travel costs are low (though if you are going outside the city limits, it is wise to agree the price of the journey before you start) — for example, from El Cortes del Inglés (Dept. Store) to the Muelle Santa Catalina will cost just under 100 pesetas (50p).

It is advisable to use a city bus when travelling between the old and new parts of Las Palmas. The main bus station in the old part is on Calle Rafael Cabrera, below Parque de San Telmo and between a street called Triana and the sea. In the new city the central stopping place for buses is in the Parque Santa Catalina.

Buses are cheap 25 pesetas (13p) and frequent between 0800 and 2000 hrs, timetables are available from the Tourist Office. There are three main bus routes covering Las Palmas:

No. 1   From the main bus station at Parque de San Telmo via Leon y Castillo and Parque Santa Catalina to the port.

No. 2   From the main bus station at Parque de San Telmo to the Cathedral and Market via Tomás Morales and Plaza Carasco.

No. 3   From the main bus station at Parque de San Telmo up the hill, past the dog racing track, Nueve Campo España, via Paseo de Chile at the back of the city to Escalerites and the port.

In fact, one of the best ways to view Las Palmas is to take the no. 3 bus, a taxi or car along the Paseo de Chil. This long road runs parallel with the Avenida Maritima on the sea front but climbs higher up above the city. winding about to give fine views of Escaleritas, the modern part of the city, and the harbour below.   Alternatively, coach tour operators have regular excursions, which can be booked at hotels or travel agents.   Tours vary from half-day shopping trips to full-day excursions to visit all the main sights in Las Palmas;   the latter include lunch.

From the Parque Santa Catalina one can make a trip in a horse-drawn carriage (*tartanas*) through the city of Las Palmas. It takes about an hour, and is a leisurely way to see the sights (arrange the price first).

City tour 1

(Vegueta, the old city — Cathedral de Santa Ana — Museo Canario — Casa de Colon — Mercado Municipal: half day, walking)

Visitors who come and go without exploring the old city will only half know Las Palmas, for the Vegueta, as it is called, is full of history, with its narrow streets and old buildings.   The towers of the **Cathedral of Santa Ana,** founded in the fifteenth century, seem to dominate the Vegueta.   Viewed from the Plaza de Santa Ana the Cathedral is mighty in appearance.   The present building, begun in the late eighteenth century, is still unfinished but there is plenty to admire and enjoy.   The Gothic interior soars high in beautiful deep arches, three central naves being the same height.   Numerous rich relics are preserved here, including the Pendon de la Conquista (Banner of Conquest) embroidered by Queen Isabella during the conquest, but sadly, today, they have to be kept locked away, to be displayed only on special occasions.

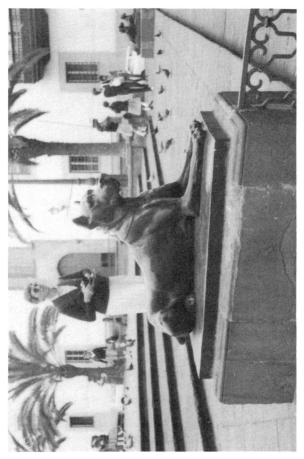

One of the wonderful black statues of huge dogs that face the Cathedral in the Plaza de Santa Ana. They represent the aboriginal wild dogs found in the island by ancient explorers and from which, from the latin 'canis', the islands derived their name.

In the palm lined Plaza de Santa Ana are statues of huge dogs representing the aboriginal dogs from which Grand Canary and the Canary Islands took their names, (*Canis* being the Latin for dog). This Plaza is the scene of the celebration of the feast of Corpus Cristi in June when the streets of the city are richly decorated with carpets of beautiful flowers and grasses, a laborious and loving work of art. A great procession leaves the Cathedral, its huge bells tolling as the great *Monstrance* (Holy Image) is held high by six men, followed by the Bishop and Church dignitaries. Flower petals rain down from the balconies above and the air is filled with sweet perfume as the procession walks over the wonderful floral carpets. Later flaming torches lead the procession back to the Cathedral and a battle of flowers and other festivities go on long into the night.

The Plaza is always full of tourists and Canarians busy with their cameras and with well-fed pigeons fluttering around. On the left, as one faces the Cathedral, is the Palacio Episcopal (Bishop's Palace) and at the far end of the Plaza de Santa Ana is the large town hall.

Nearby, on the corner of Calle Doctor Chil and Calle Doctor Vernau is the **Museo Canario** (Canary Museum). (Open from 1000 to 1300 hrs and 1500 to 1800 hrs, Saturday 1000 to 1200 hrs.) This is the most important museum on the island, and its excellent catalogue explains its purpose. The collection is divided into three sections displaying the geology, the history and pre-history of the island. The latter includes a large collection of cro-magnon relics, including lumps of solidified lava hurled out from volcanos. There are even Guanche mummies, skulls and bones, and beautiful ceramics and objects from Guanche times. There are many books and maps relating to the resistance of the heroic Guanches; the museum library contains 30,000 books on all subjects.

Turning left off Calle Doctor Chil into Plaza del Pilar Nuevo one reaches **Casa Museo de Colon** (House of Columbus) in Calle Colon. This fine fifteenth century building was the military governor's house, where Christopher Columbus stayed when he visited Las Palmas. Now restored, it is a pleasing museum to Columbus and the days of the Conquest. A cool galleried patio has an old well in the centre, with hanging ferns and potted plants. Upstairs the rooms are furnished with antiques and old tapestries, and paintings hang on the walls, some on loan from the Prado in Madrid.

Outside all is very quiet and peaceful. The narrow road which is still cobbled, leads to Iglesia San Antonio Abad, a tiny church built in 1892 on the site of the church where Columbus prayed before he set sail for the New World. Today a beautiful bougainvillea at one side of the church climbs over the roof, a much photographed splash of colour.

In the same area the city's principal market, off Leon Y Castillo, lies close to the waterfront (the main Autopista to the south passes between the market and the sea). The **Mercado Municipal** is nicknamed 'The Market of the Forty Thieves' because there are that number of stalls!

Couriers from the coach excursions warn tourists to watch their pockets and handbags, so maybe the nickname is apt. Fresh fruit, vegetables, meat, fish, household and leather goods contribute to a colourful display. One of the best buys is the *queso blanco* (goat's cheese).

City tour 2

(Triana — Parque Doramas — Pueblo Canario — Ciudad Jardin — Parque Santa Catalina: half day, walking)

Across from the market the busy highway over the Barranco de Guiniguada, leads to the district called Triana. One of the first buildings you will notice is the theatre, Teatro Perez Galdos in Calle Lentini 1. Built in 1919, it was decorated by Nestor de la Torre, the Canarian painter and sculptor who has done so much to promote the traditional Canarian style. Inside, the huge foyer is decorated with paintings of Canary fruits, the theme of the magnificently carved balustrades. Ballet, orchestral concerts and operas are performed during the winter.

Calle Mayor de Triana runs through the heart of the main shopping centre. From Triana, at the Parque de Cervantes, this road joins with Calle Leon Y Castillo. It is along this route, about two kilometres north, that the lovely **Parque Doramas** is located. This large park encloses the Santa Catalina Hotel and the **Pueblo Canario,** a model Canary Island village. The five-star eighteenth century Santa Catalina Hotel, recently refurbished, has a luxurious setting of palms and exotic shrubs. Used by visiting heads of state its gracious interior is dignified and quiet.

Las Palmas streets are always busy with shoppers looking for tax free bargains. There are also plenty of restaurants and bars.

The bougainvillea adorned tiny church of San Antonio Abad, Las
Palmas. Built in 1892 on the site of the former church where
Christopher Columbus prayed before he departed to discover the
New World.

Pueblo Canario is a reconstruction of a Canary village, built in memory of Nestor de la Torre, (1888 - 1938). The small Nestor Museum contains a collection of his works. Around a central patio, tables and chairs are set out where visitors may watch exhibitions of Canarian folk dancing and singing. Small shops selling antiques and works of local crafts people are built into alcoves around the edge of the patio. In February and March the jacaranda trees make a wonderful show with their bluish purple blossoms.

Amongst the tall palm trees and green vegetation many native specimens grow, including one of the famous dragon trees (*drago*) venerated by the Guanches. This tree looks like a relic from ancient times: the thick trunk broadens out into several massive trunks, the top being ridged with short green spiky leaves. It is sometimes called the 'dragon's blood tree', for the resinous secretions turn dark red, like blood. The park contains a small zoo, public swimming pool and tennis courts.

To one side of the Plaza de la Caleta is the Ermita de Santa Catalina, a little church dedicated to the patron saint of Mallorca in the Balearic Islands, built by Mallorquin monks in the fifteenth century. It was one of the first churches to be built on the island.

From Parque Doramas the Calle Leon Y Castillo, continues north through the wealthy residential quarter of **Ciudad Jardin** (garden city). Large houses with pretty gardens eventually give way to blocks of recently built flats as the road ends back at the **Parque Santa Catalina** and the port area.

Other places of interest

The **British Club** in Las Palmas is at 274, Leon Y Castillo. The club is open Tuesday to Saturday from 1000 to 1530 hrs and 1930 to midnight, Mondays from 1830 hrs to midnight, closed on Sundays. Lunch, dinner and snacks at the bar are reasonably priced. The atmosphere is quiet and colonial with English newspapers, magazines, periodicals, a library, two full-size snooker tables and table tennis. Video films, dinner dances, barbecues, curry evenings and a flourishing bridge section make it a pleasant venue. Temporary membership can be had, minimum one week, maximum six months. The fine old building is an example from the past glories of colonial prosperity. When you go inside have a look at the old photograph which shows the house when it was surrounded by fields.

The **British American Clinic,** 5 Sagusta, Puerto de la Luz, gives a 24-hour emergency service, with ambulance. Chemists (*farmacia*), as in all Canarian towns, display a green Maltese Cross outside, illuminated at night. A notice shows which chemists are open at night.

The **Anglican Church** in Las Palmas is the Holy Trinity Church, Calle Rafael Ramirez, Ciudad Jardin. Holy Communion is at 0800 and 1200 hrs, Matins at 1100 hrs. Mass at the **Roman Catholic Columbus Church,** is at 1030 hrs. The **Baptist Church,** Ingeniero, Salinas 17, is near to the Alcaravaneras Beach; services on Sunday are at 1100 and 1800 hrs.

Island tour 1

(Las Palmas — Aeropuerto de Gando — Carrizal — Ingenio — Arinaga — San Agustin: about 70 km; full day by car)

Most visitors to Gran Canaria tour in a clockwise direction. This is probably because they are in a hurry to see the warmer part of the island which is in the south.

The southern exit route from Las Palmas is well signposted from the outskirts of the city. If in the centre of town, make for the seafront and Avenida Maritima, pass the Naval Base and the Real Club Náutico de Gran Canaria (the yacht club) and head south. The traffic moves fast in a three-lane rush for a few kilometres, following very close to the sea, giving clear views of the harbour. Near the sixteenth century fortress of San Cristobel, where old fishermen's houses are seen at the water's edge, the road narrows, then turns into the motorway, Autopista Sud. Travel is fast and rather dull, for the land is dry and featureless except for the cacti that thrive in the arid volcanic soil. On the sea side of the road a few small clusters of houses are to be seen along dusty roads.

A turning inland towards Jinamar leads to **Telde,** an industrial town of importance where a great number of Canarians live who work in Las Palmas. Many factories provide work and help the island economy. Textile, furniture, engineering, chemical and fish canning works are to be seen on industrial estates. Banana packing stations and areas cultivated with cucumbers under plastic greenhouses add nothing to the beauty of the landscape. Telde has not succumbed to the tourist and goes about its daily business with very few visitors along the streets. Only the more venturesome and thrifty will visit the weekly outdoor market to find goods much cheaper than in the coastal towns. The parish church of San Juan Bautiste dates from the fifteenth century. It contains a beautiful Flemish reredos. The figure of Christ over the high altar is said to be the work of Tabasco Indians.

It is necessary to look further inland to where the high range of central mountains form distant peaks of reddish brown, to find real beauty in this desert like countryside. About five kilometres from Telde is the site of an old Guanche cave, Cuatro Puertas (four doors). The cave has four openings which lead into a large central cavern, which it is believed was used as a council chamber by the Guanches. The east face of the mountain is honeycombed with caves once used by the Guanches as burial chambers.

Rejoining the Autopista, roads turn seawards to the fishing villages of **La Estralla** and **Melenara.** At **Playa del Hombre** a small *urbanización,* mainly for Scandinavians, mingles with the Canarian population.

Aeropuerto de Gando, 19 kms south of Las Palmas, is conveniently situated for the city and the tourist centres in the south. The large modern building is clean and efficient with plenty of toilet facilities. There is a large parking space for long or short stay where taxis, buses and coaches arrive constantly. Inside you will find a gift shop, car rent firms and information desk where incoming passengers can find lists of available accommodation. Upstairs, a large restaurant and bar overlooks the runways. A special note is that departing tourists can buy the island grown flowers, suitably packaged for air travellers. Roses, carnations and strelitza will be gift wrapped as required. The strelitza (bird-of-paradise flowers) are especially suitable as they will last up to three weeks in water. The waxy blue and orange flowers give the illusion of a birds eye, and are very striking in appearance.

The Autopista continues on past the airport for only 20 km, road then splits into two almost parallel roads. The one which runs by the sea is a fast dual carriageway. The second road, C812, is of more interest as it goes inland enabling you to visit several busy Canarian towns.

At **Carrizal** the Artesania La Molina (the windmill), a school of needlework is open to visitors. Girls are seen at work on the *Calados,* which is a fine embroidery of drawn thread work, used for mats, tablecloths and clothes. From an early age, young girls are taught very intricate sewing. Much embroidery work is done in Canarian country homes during the summer months, when women have finished working in the fields on the tomato crops that grow from October to April.

Ingenio used to be an old colonial town with sugar cane crops, (*ingenio* means sugar plantation). Now it, too, has a school of needlework open to the public.

Aguimes is the next town south, nearby there is a large satellite tracking station. A little further inland at **Lomo de los Laetreros** is an archaeological site with stone inscriptions and designs, some clearly representing people and animals. Some hieroglyphics, similar to those found in the island of El Hierro, remain a mystery as to their meaning.

Arinaga is a small port used to export local produce; close by is a light industry estate. **Vecindario** and **El Doctoral** are well populated Canarian towns, not catering for the tourists, so the shops provide commodities usually at lower prices than in the coastal resorts. These would be useful places to find a motor engineer or to have a repair job done.

The C812 joins the coastal road again by the sea at the **Aero Club de Canaria.** Now the road approaches the great tourist area of the south and, as if by magic, gone are the dusty bare expanses, all hidden by apartments and villas. *Urbanizacións* as these complexes are called, have sprung up like mushrooms in the past ten years.

As the road winds near the coast, on both sides of the road civilisation has taken over in a big way. Some of the *urbaniz-acións* have been designed in an artistic manner and have names like 'Canary Village' and 'Sun Valley', others have fallen foul of the economic times and have not been completed. Looking very forlorn, the half built edifices stand deserted and dreary.

It is at **San Agustin,** 25 kilometres south of the airport, with its sandy plays, that the whole area starts to be fully developed.

Island tour 2

(San Agustin — Playa del Inglés — Playa de Maspalomas: distance direct about 10 km; full day by bus or car, and walking)

At the quieter end of the tourist coast, San Agustin has a casino which is part of the Hotel Tamarindos, with its own entrance from the road at Playa San Agustin. The casino is open from 2000 to 0300 hrs except Saturdays when the hours are from 2100 to 0400; closed Sunday evening. A passport is necessary to gain admission and gentlemen are expected to wear a jacket and tie. Games include French and American roulette, blackjack, chemin de fer and punto y banca. Gambling is strictly controlled by a government representative on duty throughout the evening. Admission is 400 pesetas (£2).

With its high class hotels, situated close to the sea, San Agustin caters for selective tourists. The Hotel Costa Canaria is a typical four-star establishment, with 140 twin-bedded rooms, 6 single rooms, 5 suites and three beach bungalows. All rooms have a bath, shower and wc, telephone, piped music and balcony, most with seaview or overlooking tropical gardens and the swimming pools. Tennis courts adjoin the sun lounge patios. The hotel has three bars, an elegant dining room and lounge. The midday buffet is served in the gardens. Music for dancing is played each evening. The nightclub, La Gruta Pirata is next door. It is a hotel where one is expected to be well dressed, but long dresses and dinner jackets are not obligatory in the evening.

It is worth noting that it is permissible to buy drinks at a supermarket to take to your room but they must not be consumed anywhere else in the hotel.

A new shopping centre has recently been opened at San Agustin; built on three floors it includes restaurants, bars, cafés, supermarkets, tourist shops, ironmonger, newsagents, boutiques, hairdressing salon and public toilets.

Down on the seafront it is possible to walk for several kilometres along a promenade that borders streets of villas and bungalows, many with colourful gardens. This part of the coast is favoured by wind surfing enthusiasts, the bright sails and graceful movement on the blue sea, giving vivid splashes of colour.

From San Agustin the main highway runs into **Playa del Inglés/Maspalomas,** the main tourist area of Gran Canaria. This is the boom town of the Canaries. Fifteen years ago it was an isolated fishing village with a lighthouse on the edge of the sand dunes. Gradually Europeans, especially Germans and Scandinavians, realised how magnificent the climate remained all year round. So it started with villas and bungalows, then hotels and apartment blocks were built, and more and more land was developed. Now it is a vast vacation land, its six kilometres of golden sands, warm sea waters and constant sunshine providing a holiday paradise. Endless cafés, bars and restaurants cater for every nationality and taste. Dancing, discos, night clubs, dog racing, bingo and sports of every kind can be enjoyed at Playa del Inglés and Maspalomas; you may have a camel ride!

A comfortable way of exploring part of Playa del Inglés is to take the 'Mini Train' from outside the Supermarket El Veril in Avenida Italia, which leaves every half hour from 1000 to 1200 hrs and 1600 to 2200 hrs. This little train runs along the main streets and has open carriages, the journey takes 50 minutes and costs 200 pesetas (£1), children half-price.

Another method of getting about for those who do not have a driving licence and do not wish to walk, is to hire a bicycle or moped. Prices for the latter, including insurance, fuel and tax is 1050 pesetas (£5.40 per day) or 4650 pesetas (£24 per week). Supermarkets, travel agents and rent-a-car firms abound in Playa del Inglés, many are attached to hotels. Shopping centres (called *commercials*) are grouped conveniently. One built like an Arab *souk* is called El Kasbah and has many African and Indian traders who will enjoy bartering for your custom.

For many the greatest attraction of all is the wonderful beach. Every morning it is a fascinating sight to see hordes of tourists of all shapes, sizes and nationalities emerge from hundreds of apartments, villas and hotels all making for the beach. No wonder, for the sands are soft and clean and the sea is mostly calm and safe for swimming. Layout chairs with sunshades are for hire, beach cafés can provide full meals and drinks. A large free car park is right by the sea. Each day vast numbers walk the sands, in the morning going westwards towards the sand dunes; at midday the stream returns, only to be repeated in the afternoon, an almost continuous procession of bodies all aiming to get as tanned as possible.

Nowadays the Spanish authorities acquiesce to the demand for naturist sunbathing. At Playa del Inglés the western end of the beach has notice boards proclaiming that nudism is permitted. This mainly takes place amongst the sand dunes. The very hardy walkers will stride out as far as **Playa de Maspalomas,** eight kilometres away, have their lunch at a beach bar, then return to Playa del Inglés in the afternoon. Quite an energetic way to spend a day or even if one does have dips in the sea to cool down.

Take care that you do not get sunburn here. Another point regarding health is drinking water. Because of the water shortage, especially in Playa del Inglés, the addition of chemicals is for purification tends to give drinking water a strong and unpleasant taste. It is wiser to drink bottled water, such as *Firgas* which is available in supermarkets at 30-70 pesetas (15p-35p) a bottle, aerated or still.

Amongst the many hotels in Playa del Inglés the three star Hotel Eugenia Victoria, Avenida Gran Canaria 26 is a comfortable friendly place. Conveniently situated it has a free bus service to and from the beach. There are 400 twin bedded rooms, all with sitting room and modern bathroom, telephone and piped music, and balconies overlooking the gardens and swimming pools. All the public rooms are airconditioned: spacious restaurant, lounge, and cocktail bar. There is dancing to a live band, TV and a card room. The pleasant grounds include, as well as swimming pools, two tennis courts, petanca and table tennis. A shopping area contains a hairdresser, souvenir shop, boutique and rent-a-car firm. Of special interest is a Canarian wood carver who works in his shop carving walnut and olivewood, making intricate and lifelike statues. In the same avenue as the Hotel Eugenia Victoria is the singular looking Hotel Waikiki, built in circular towers with a large totem pole outside the entrance. Both the Eugenia Victoria and the Waikiki have English-speaking public relations representatives who are ready to assist with any queries.

Playa del Inglés abounds with restaurants, cafes and bars dispensing food suitable for all nationalities. Service is good. The majority of establishments have live or taped music and a wide range of night life to suit all ages and tastes is at hand.

Many and varied are the coach excursions from Playa del Inglés. All the hotels have a list of departure times, itineraries and prices. Couriers will advise and are often informative about local events. Travel agents (*viajes*) such as Ultramar Express SA and Insular SA run regular sight seeing trips. Make sure that you book a coach which has an English-speaking guide. A half day sightseeing trip to Las Palmas from Playa del Inglés costs about 725 pesetas (£3.70); a tour of the island, full day, 1,400 pesetas (£7.20); and a donkey safari, full day, including food, 2,500 pesetas (£13). A visit to Aladino's Nightclub includes dinner, dancing and two floorshows, 2475 pesetas (£13).

The majority of tourists in Playa del Inglés, and elsewhere on the islands are Germans, so much of the publicity is geared for their requirements.

One of the most suitable places for family entertainment is the Wild West village of Sioux City. In the Canon del Aguila, well signposted on the main San Agustin to Playa del Inglés road, an old film set is now used for a Wild West show. Visitors can see great feats of horsemanship, knife throwing, lassoing from horseback, a 'bank robbery', cattle-herding and many other exciting daredevil deeds.

Tourists can walk up the main street of this cowboy village and visit Western-style bars and shops, church and corals. In the 'hotel' meals and drinks are served. Open from 1000 hrs, shows at 1200 and 1530 hrs. Several nights a week 'barbecue parties' are held: entrance cost includes whisky, chicken, pork chops, steaks, potatoes, salad, plus a banana! Later there is a sparkling show by Tom Leddas and family, Mexicans of great daring and skill. Free drinks and dancing continue until midnight.

Between Playa del Inglés and Playa de Maspalomas is the Maspalomas Golf Club. There are two 18-hole courses at Par 71 and Par 73. It is remarkable that this should be here, set in an area of moving sand dunes. With its palm trees, grassy lawns and numerous lakes the club has become one of Spain's most popular courses. Hiring of equipment is no problem, green fees cost 1200 pesetas (£6.18). After palying there is ample opportunity for refreshment in the swimming pool and the luxurious bar restaurant.

Lucha Canaria is the oldest and most typical sport in Gran Canaria with its tradition rooted in the island's pre history. It is a form of wrestling practised in towns and villages. Matches take place in a special arena at **El Tablero** a few kilometres south of Playa del Inglés. Announcements of times appear in the Spanish newspapers and on posters.

In the same vicinity is found the Plaza de Toros (bull ring). In Gran Canaria these events are billed as 'bull fight parties' because the bulls are not killed. Costing 900 pesetas (£4.60) per person, tickets can be obtained at travel agents and hotel receptions.

For nature lovers and the family, the **Palmitos Park,** open 0930 to 1900 hrs, provides a gentle pleasure. In a sub-tropical oasis 45 different species of palm trees grow amongst gardens and lakes. It is said that 1200 exotic birds live there; some are caged but over 400 fly freely, the flamingoes being especially beautiful. Every day there are 25-minute long shows when ten parrots entertain with marvellous tricks. There is also an excellent collection of cacti and agaves. A regular bus service goes to the Palmitos Park from Playa del Inglés.

Newly opened and close to the main road just north of Playa del Inglés and Maspalomas is a 'go kart' track (open from 1000 to 2300 hrs); there are karts for all ages, plus two bars, a restaurant and games room.

The Faro (lighthouse) at Playa de Maspalomas is a centuries-old beacon which gives a welcome light to passing shipping. Close by luxury hotels, apartments and a small shopping centre enable tourists to enjoy a holiday right by the edge of the sea. An oasis-like combination of palms, lagoon and sand dunes has attracted unique flora and fauna, also vast numbers of migrating birds. Maspalomas means literally 'more pigeons'. The human species can enjoy near-perfect sunbathing and swimming — a red flag flies when the undercurrents are dangerous. The more energetic can ride a horse, even a camel, on a safari excursion, or quietly fish in the lagoon.

Island tour 3

(Playa de Maspalomas — Arguineguin — Puerto Rico: about 18 km; half day by bus or car)

At the road junction, where the main road C182 turns westwards from Maspalomas, a Texaco petrol filling station provides a 24-hour service but is closed on Sundays. Following the main coastal route westwards the countryside remains bare and arid, and the central mountains are still to be seen inland. Despite the poor soil, it is in this part of Gran Canaria that huge crops of outdoor tomatoes are grown, the bamboo canes supporting them standing in near-perfect straight rows. In the past tomatoes have made an important contribution to the economy and, despite the great tourist invasion, are still grown in vast quantities. Conditions for a lot of the workers are still primitive, many living in what are virtually shacks in 'shanty towns', the children running barefoot and whole families work in the fields. Irrigation is by a series of water channels that are strictly controlled, often by just a dam of mud. The precious water is piped from the high mountains and retained in reservoirs. During the winter months the Canarians look longingly for rain whenever a few clouds gather, while tourists invariably hope for sunshine! An interesting fact is that because the tomato crop is picked for export when green, it is not always easy to buy ripe tomatoes in the shops.

Amongst the tomato fields and about 2 kms from the Texaco petrol station, a turning seawards down a rough unmade road leads to **Melonares Playa.** A privately-owned beach open to the public, it has a small seaside bar that serves lunches at tables on the sands. Most of the year the beach has plenty of sand and provides splendid swimming, and it is popular with windsurfers. During the winter months when gales out in the Atlantic can send in huge waves, it has happened that the sand has been washed away leaving only rocks and pebbles; luckily the sand returns. This beach is a favourite haunt for motor-caravanners who, during the winter months love to find a peaceful venue close to the sea.

A further kilometre or so west at **Pasito Blanco** is a newly-built marine harbour, the Puerto de Club de Yates, a yacht club with modern facilities including apartments, ships' chandler and post office.

The main highway continues to wind its way very close to the sea, and some of the bends require careful attention. Approaching **Arguineguin,** there is a large cement factory built out on a jetty; the bay is always busy with shipping. In the same area, behind concrete walls, a banana plantation stretches either side of the road.

Arguineguin, once a sleepy fishing village, is now developing into an important fishing port. Several good supermarkets, a petrol station, a camping Gaz stockist, post office and restaurants have encouraged tourists to aid and expand the growth. Yet, to day, it has managed to retain its original Canarian character. The Tuesday open air market is a meeting place for locals and holiday makers who mingle cheerfully.

The winding coastal road continues on past modern urbanizatións of apartments, some luxurious and attractive, their balconies ablaze with geraniums and bougainvillea. All have their own swimming pools and supermarkets.

Going through a short tunnel the road reaches **Puerto Rico,** a man-made oasis built entirely for the tourist. Sand was brought from the Sahara Desert to make a beach. This sheltered bay has perhaps the most favourable climate in all Gran Canaria and its theme is luxury, leisure and sport. Indeed, during January and February, the coolest months, coach loads of tourists are brought daily from Las Palmas, where it can be cloudy and cool, to enjoy Puerto Rico's sunshine. Consequently the tiny beach becomes packed with bodies, but it has a happy carefree atmosphere.

On either side of the hills that surround Puerto Rico, hundreds of apartments are set in long terraces, with roads running down to the beach below. In the centre of Puerto Rico are parks that are a sheer joy — a profusion of ornamental trees and tropical shrubs. Green grass grows as if by magic in the dry soil and paths wind under exotic trees, as in a fairytale garden. Carparks, swimming pools, tennis courts and restaurants have been planned into this colourful plantation.

Puerto Rico harbour where shark fishing excursions are very much enjoyed by those who like a sea trip with food, champagne and swimming — with a shark being caught too!

A *centro commercial* (shopping precinct) has open-fronted shops selling a varied range of tourist requirements and souvenirs. Leather and brasswork from Africa; transistors, watches and cameras from Japan; ceramics and textiles from Spain; jewellery, silver, gold and porcelain all mingle with cheap toys and ornaments to lure the pesetas from your pocket.

Nearer the beach by the busy roads that criss-cross in the centre of Puerto Rico, are the banks, post office and telephones. An underpass tunnel is helpful when the roads are busy. Supermarkets, self-drive car rentals, travel agents, newsagents and many boutiques can be found here.

Two roads lead to two separate harbours, both used by yachts and private pleasure boats. At **Puerto Nuevo** the new port, two old red-sailed sailing ships, the 'Gefion' and the 'San Miguel' make daily tourist excursions out to sea, except Mondays. The full-day trip includes a meal with wine and entertainment, an opportunity to swim and assist with sailing the ship. A day at sea is also offered in the motor vessels 'Hai Turn' and 'Alexandria', when shark fishing can be part of the day's fun. Shorter trips can be made on the 'Sea Safari', which offers a two-hour trip along the coast. During this excursion fresh fish is barbecued and wine drunk; the crew say anyone can go with them — except pirates!

Puerto Rico has acquired fame all over the world as a big game fishing centre. For centuries fishermen have been chasing tuna, bonita, shark, barracuda and swordfish. Nowadays amateur sports fishermen as well as professionals participate, and nothing is more exciting than to be on the quay at Puerto Rico between 1530 and 1630 hrs, when the powerful little fishing boats return, and everyone is eager to see the day's catch being sorted, weighed and often photographed. Fishermen exchange stories, tourists gaze in amazement and waiters start laying tables in the restaurants. Puerto Rico has many restaurants that specialise in international cooking, but the fresh fish is the best.

There are no night clubs in Puerto Rico but several restaurants have music and dancing and some of the apartments have discos. Successful wind surfing, water ski and sailing schools operate in the harbour, the calm waters being ideal for beginners.

Island tour 4

(Puerto Rico — Tauro — Mogan — San Nicolás — Puerto de las Nieves: about 95 km; half day by car)

Still travelling clockwise your road out of Puerto Rico leads alongside the sea and a series of small coves to**Playa de Tauro,** where the only permanent camping site in Gran Canaria is situated. Recently extended it is now in three parts. The original camp on the sea side of the road is right by the beach, which is part sand, part pebble. Used mainly by back-packers and small motorcaravans, it is where the younger element of campers gather. On the main road a restaurant recently opened is proving very popular. Good quality meals well served are reasonably priced.

On the inland side of the road, behind concrete walls, the main camp has marked pitches, plenty of shade, modern toilets, cold showers, washing sinks and chemical toilet disposal, electric points and lights at night until 2300 hrs. A security guard patrols the camps.

A third part of the camp is 3 km up the *barranco* (valley) in a lovely setting of craggy mountains and eucalyptus trees. A level sheltered site, it has modern toilets, cold showers, washing sinks and a swimming pool. At the bar individual meals are prepared. Geraldo and Geraldine, both Canarians, work hard to ensure that all campers are happy, their cheerful smiles of greeting makes everyone welcome. The sites are owned by Señor Martin Suarez from Las Palmas, who visits regularly to see that all is well. He hopes to continue to enlarge and improve the camps. He is ably assisted by Señor Santiago and his friendly family plus a large contingent of Alsatian dogs.

In the *barrancos* near Tauro, small *urbanizacións* of bungalows and villas are occupied by foreigners, some all the year round though the majority only during the winter months by those who enjoy a warm climate.

The valleys also contain Canarian homesteads where chickens, tomatoes and avocado trees give life to the dry landscape. Fields of bananas and aubergines help to provide an income for those Canarians who still resist the temptation of the tourist trade and prefer to work the land.

A small German owned hotel, The Rivera, is situated in the next bay. As well as beach bathing it has a swimming pool and is open to non-residents.

140

The C812 road continues to hug the coast, winding in a spectacular corniche. The road surface is good but care is required on the bends. There are lovely views of mountains and small sandy coves, rock and pebble beaches, which one can walk down to.

At one such bay, **Taurito,** there is a dusty, sandy sheltered beach, privately owned but open to the public, and popular with nudist bathers. Some attempt has been made to landscape the area with trees and shrubs, consequently it is sometimes frequented by birds such as the spectacular hoopoe, whose crest, long curved bill, light pinky brown plumage and striking black and white wing pattern make it easy to identify.

At **Puerto de Mogan,** in the south west, you find yourself at a busy fishing village in a fertile valley. Until recent years Puerto de Mogan could only be reached by sea, and the extension of the coastal road has considerably altered the village. Nowadays TV aerial masts are seen at the tope of the high cliffs reaching down to the cluster of houses below. The harbour is being enlarged and the quaint little fish restaurants are becoming larger and more tourist orientated with menus outside in several languages. It is still a pleasant place with a relaxed atmosphere.

The road now turns inland, becoming narrower and going up the *barranco* between fields of crops. It climbs steadily into the mountains for some 9 kilometres to the village of **Mogan.** Set on the mountainside, this typically Canarian *pueblo* has only a sprinkling of foreign residents. A few tourist shops and bars are easily located. Being well above sea level, Mogan is favoured by a little rainfall each year and a moisture climate, hence the cultivation. In the gardens oranges, lemons, grapefruit, papaya and coffee grow well. Tall palms and vivid shrubs like bougainvillea, poinsettia and geraniums all make it an attractive place.

Leaving Mogan the road improves; a newly constructed two-lane highway winds on up into the mountains, giving panoramic views of much beauty. Strata of volcanic rock create spectacular shapes and sizes, quite awesome, overpowering even. The completion of this piece of roadwork, has made it possible to drive in a complete circle round the island.

San Nicolás is 29 kms beyond Mogan, spread out in a fertile, flat region by the sea, intensively cultivated with fields of tomatoes, cucumbers and beans under plastic. Some sugar cane is still grown there.

San Nicolás de Tolentino is a tiny scattering of houses by a shingle beach, **Punta de la Aldea.** A few small boats go inshore fishing each day and sometimes it is possible to buy fresh fish outside the bar-restaurant that lies beside the main road. Fresh fish is never cheap as the demand is so high from the Canarians.

The C810 road now climbs very steeply, twisting and winding its way northwards to Puerto de las Nieves, 44 km away. Often the sea is turquoise blue with good views over the Atlantic. On clear days the peak of Mount Teide on Tenerife is seen, snow capped and amazingly beautiful, a perfect cone of white in the blue sky. Time is needed to drive along this stretch of road, for the countryside is wild, with little habitation, and many twists and bends have unguarded edges that drop sharply away to the sea.

Island tour 5

(Puerto de las Nieves — Agaete — Los Berrazales — Sardina — Galdar — Guia — Las Palmas: about 63 km; half way by car)

The **Agaete** Valley of **Los Berrazales** is one of the most fertile in Gran Canaria, just 7 kms in length; the moist air from the surrounding mountains creates a green 'Garden of Eden' which is a pleasure to behold, especially if one has been staying in the sunbaked, arid south. Grass grows amongst wild geraniums, marigolds and dogroses along the verges. The aroma of pine trees, jasmine and honeysuckle sweetens the air and tall palm trees stand out picturesquely against the reddish cultivated soil.

At the end of the narrow valley ferruginous water tumbles down from the mountainside. Once there was a *Banos de Agaete,* a hotel where rheumatic sufferers could bathe in the waters, but sadly its doors are now closed. However mineral water is still bottled at a small factory and delivered all over the island.

Halfway along the valley, one is surprised to see Casa Romantica, a bar-restaurant of exceptionally high standard. Owned by Senor Bruckman, born a Swiss but now a naturalised Canarian, who presides over his immaculate establishment. The cuisine is of an international standard, at appropriate prices. It is a place much favoured by families from Las Palmas, and not on the usual tourist route. Señor Bruckman has created around his Swiss chalet style restaurant a small plantation of exotic plants — brilliant double red poinsettas, bougainvillea, roses, carnations, strelitzia, hibiscus; towering above are huge rubber trees; papaya, avocado, palms, shrubs of coffee and rosemary mix with orange, lemon, grapfruit and mango trees. Amongst all this profusion is a small zoo, where monkeys and rare birds are lovingly housed. Early in the morning as the mist rises from the mountain tops surrounding the valley, one hears wild bird song mingling with the bells of the goats as they graze the steep slopes — it seems like a tropical Switzerland!

Well worth a visit are the **Cuevas de las Cruces,** 5 kms north of Agaete. These caves have been inhabited since ancient times and remain cool in summer and warm in winter. The ownership of a cave is closely guarded by the family who pass it on to the next generation.

At a junction 5 kms north of the caves, the road turns westwards to the coast and **Sardina,** set amid acres of banana plantations. Sardina houses a small community of Canarians who mostly work on the plantations or make a living by fishing from the tiny port. A small hotel on the seafront is closed during the winter.

The next town is **Galdar** on the north coast which, with neighbouring **Guia** is of some historical importance. Galdar was the capital of the Guanche Kingdom and some Guanche relics are preserved in the town hall, which is opposite the church in the Plaza Mayor, (main square), which also houses an ancient dragon tree. Both these towns are agricultural centres, amid vineyards and banana plantations, and heavily populated with Canarians. Worth a visit if you can find a carpark. The *queso* (cheese) of the area is famous: *queso de flor* (flower cheese) is made from goats milk and thistle flowers.

It is just a few kilometres on the coast road from Guia to the **Cenobio de Valeron,** a notable archaeological site where hundreds of caves are to be seen in the cliff face. The place has an eerie atmosphere. It is thought to have been a convent where Guanche maidens worshipped a divinity called Alcorac. During the Spanish invasion the caves became a Guanche refuge and look-out post over the surrounding countryside.

Just beyond Guia the main road becomes a fast two-lane highway which keeps close to the coast. It gives good views of the Atlantic and the cultivated areas of the north of Gran Canaria, with dark *barrancos* making deep indentations into the central mountains. Past **Banadero** the road reaches the city of Las Palmas, and the circular tour is complete.

Inland route 1

(Moya — Firgas — Balcon de Zamora — Teror — Arucas —
Las Palmas; about 77 km; half day drive)

An alternative route from Guia to Las Palmas can be enjoyed by
taking the road to **Moya,** which affords a scenic drive into the
green north of Gran Canaria, where fields of corn and grazing
cattle mingle with vines and potato crops. Heavy oxen till the
soil, the small farmhouses are pretty with white wash and
flowers. Carnations grow well here and are produced
commercially.

Moya is a spread-out town perched on the edge of a steep
barranco, the huge twin towers of its church making a striking
picture from a distance. The stronghold of the last Guanche
King, Doramas, it is also the birthplace of Tomas Morales, the
Canarian poet (1885 to 1921).

The road continues to twist and turn up and down *barrancos*
sometimes in a pine forest, then by a river bed. A fork left leads
to **Firgas,** famous for its spring waters, which are bottled and
sold throughout the Canary Islands. The mineral water is sold
as *con gas* and *sin gas* (still). The bottling plant is out of the
village on the road to Vallesco. At the **Balcon de Zamora** on the
Vallesco road a view-point allows an extensive vista of the fertile
green valley below. A large restaurant, much used by coach
tours, serves freshly cooked meals. *Tapas* (snacks) can be had
at the bar.

The same road, now climbs higher and higher through a
series of pine forest to the centre of the island and Cruz de
Tejeda. But our route takes us just six kilometres down a zig
zag road to the important town of **Teror** set in a peaceful valley.
The major point of interest is the large Canarian church of
Nuestra Senora del Pino. This splendid shrine draws great
numbers of the faithful, especially on 8th September when the
Fiesta de la Virgen del Pino takes place. She takes her name
from the pine tree that fell when the Virgin Mary is said to have
made an appearance to the priest of the village. The beautiful
alabaster image is enthroned in the church, which dates from
1767. Richly dressed in heavily embroidered robes, the image
is set on high, surrounded by cherubs, holding incense bowls.
The wonderful silver canopy is said to be the work of a celebrated eighteenth century silversmith from Tenerife.

Teror is a delightful Canarian town with carved pine balconies
along its quiet streets. In the large square outside the church
are several small tourist shops. Some of the embroidered
needlework and lace is made by the nuns at the local convent. If
you are looking for an heirloom the work is exquisite.

144

Just across the square from the church is the House of the Patrons of Our Lady of the Pines, an old Canarian mansion open to the public, the house has belonged to the family of Manrique de la Lara (a noble surname) since the seventeenth century and is still used by the family for summer holidays. It contains valuable silver and glassware, furniture and ornaments.

From Teror it is fifteen kilometres north via El Palmar to **Arucas** which is the third largest town, eighteen kilometres from Las Palmas, set in a fertile plain with important banana plantations stretching in all directions. Montana de Arucas, an old volcanic cone, affords fine views of the town and the north coast as far as Las Palmas. An outstanding feature of Arucas is the parish church, St. Juan Bautista, more like a cathedral. Although built as recently as 1909, the Gothic style gives it a much older appearance. Many fine old colonial houses are to be seen in Arucas which has busy streets and a large municipal car park.

To get the feel of the island go into one of the small bars in the town and have a coffee or something stronger. Order a doughnut filled with custard cream, or something savoury such as *tortilla* (Spanish omelette) or *papas arrugadas*, the baby Canarian potatoes and eaten with the local piquant sauce *mojo*, which is made from peppers, oil, vinegar and spices. It is perfectly acceptable for unaccompanied females to use the bars. Often one sees quite young children with their mothers, enjoying a coke and crisps.

Excursion parties visiting Arucas are taken around a banana plantation, with a guide to explain the development of the plant in all stages of its growth. Visitors are able to purchase bananas fresh from the trees. Arucas is also the centre of the rum industry. This spirit, made from the locally grown cane, is very popular with Canarians.

The journey from Arucas to Las Palmas on the C810 is only eighteen kilometres but because the road winds through several *barrancos* with many undulations and in some places is narrow, allow yourself about an hour to reach the city. Driving through Tenoya and Tamaraceite you will see more fertile banana plantations, which continue to the outskirts of Las Palmas city.

Inland route 2

(Las Palmas — Jardin Botanico Canario — Monte Cello — Caldera Bandama — Santa Brigida — San Mateo — Pozo de las Nieves — Cruz de Tejeda — Las Palmas: about 94 km return; full day by car)

From Las Palmas it is only thirty five kilometres to the centre of the island and its highest point, Pozo de las Nieves, 1392 m. From Las Palmas take the C811, a fast motorway, for about seven kilometres to **Tafira Baja,** which is really a continuation of Las Palmas city, and contains many expensive houses belonging to its prosperous businessmen.

Jardin Botanico Canario, the botanical gardens, are about eleven kilometres west of Las Palmas, along this road in the direction of Santa Brigida. There is free entrance into these important botanical gardens, situated in an area called Angostura. Open 1000 to 1200 and 1500 to 1800 hrs.

The beautiful Angostura Valley has an ideal climate for growing rare botanical species and the gardens contain a fine collection of native flora, including trees recently planted (1964) which have reached a great height. Represented here is the Canary laurel (Laurisilva), which has a slender trunk, light grey bark and dark green leathery leaves. These can be used as a spice, though they are not so flavoursome as the genuine laurel (sweet bay) leaves.

In the same area is **Monte Cello,** the island's best wine producing region — *vino tinto de Monte* is pleasant and well-known local red wine.

From the C811 a detour is recommended to visit the **Caldera Bandama,** one of the wonders of Gran Canaria. This volcanic crater, some 609 m above sea level, has a peaceful green bowl 198 m deep and over a kilometre wide, with a flourishing farm at the bottom. Incidentally it is only possible to descend to the bottom on foot or by donkey. The Mirador de Bandama at the top of a high cone of land gives magnificent views in all directions, out to the mighty Atlantic and towards the centre and south of the island.

Nearby is the Club de Golf de las Palmas, 14 kms from Las Palmas, founded in 1891. It has an 18-hole course open all the year round, except Good Friday and visitors are welcome. Those staying at the Club Inn pay half the stipulated green fee of 250 pesetas (£1.30) on weekdays and 450 pesetas (£2.30) on Sundays and holidays. There is a bar restaurant and horse-riding is available.

At La Atalaya, are more Guanche caves, some quite close to the road, which are still in everyday use as homes and for storage. It is said that there are over one thousand caves here; a nearby centre for ceramics and basket work is useful for souvenir shopping.

Rejoining the C811 road it is a pleasant drive towards **Santa Brigida** through green hills and valleys, especially beautiful in February when the odd rain shower freshens the countryside and emphasises the sweet perfume of the almond blossom. The road winds its way in ever increasing height until it reaches **San Mateo** at 650 m. This village has a popular tourist attraction, the Casa de Cho Zacarias, an old farmhouse made into a rural museum. Typical rustic implements and Canary furniture are on show, and in a *bodega* visitors can sample the local cheese and wine. On Sundays a busy open air market attracts both tourists and Canarians; sales include live animals, especially goats.

Through an area of upland agriculture the road continues towards the mountain peaks. A turning off the main road leads almost to the top of the **Pozo de las Nieves** 1950 m affording wonderful views in a quiet and tranquil setting. In the distance can be seen the Roque Nublo, (*nube* means cloud) a peak once held sacred by the Guanches and still awe-inspiring.

Cruz de Tejeda, accepted as the centre of the island, lies inland at a height of 1450 m. The Cross of Tejeda was a crucifix originally made of pine, it has now been replaced by a cross made of island stone. It stands in a square where tourist coaches park. Old men with bedecked donkeys tempt tourists to have a ride; beware, these genial old men will offer to use your camera to photograph you and your friends beside their donkey and expect payment! Small stalls, bars and a restaurant offer a wide selection of tourist gifts, a little more expensive than elsewhere, but for the tourist in a hurry it is a good place to buy things. The fruit and vegetables on sale are of the best quality; look for the really enormous avocado pears and local goat's cheese.

When standing near the Cruz de Tejeda one is unable to see any clear views because the area around is heavily forested. However a short walk down the road leads to gaps in the trees where, when the weather is clear the views are extensive, looking over the high rock formations of the mountains of Gran Canaria and the distant snow peak of Mount Teide on Tenerife.

Inland route 3

(Cruz de Tejeda — Artenara — Pinar de Tamadaba — Cruz de Tejeda: about 64 km return; 3 hours by car)

If you wish to explore further when at Cruz de Tejeda, a winding road north west leads towards Artenara and Pinar de Tamadaba, providing a splendid drive with open views over mountains. After a short distance it enters an area of volcanic *malpais* (wasteland). Trees are now being planted here to join up with the natural forest of Tamadaba.

Artenara is the highest village on the island, at 1219 m, and it existed even before the Spanish invasion. Archeological discoveries have been made here and it has its share of caves, the Cuevas de Acusa, once Guanche strongholds. Many cave dwellings are still occupied.

The **Parador de la Silla,** close to Artenara, is one of Gran Canaria's most delightful features. A hall carved out of the rock leads to a restaurant located on a partially sheltered platform, from where there is a breathtaking view of the entire central mountain range. One should not forget to visit the chapel of Artenara's patron saint, the Virgen de Cuevita.

Pinar de Tamadaba is Gran Canaria's best known primeval forest, situated at an elevation of 1300 m and hidden in the central mountains. High and lonely, these wonderful forests consisting almost entirely of Pinus Canariensis (Canary Pine) a tree found only in the Canaries. The trees, which often grow to a height of more than thirty metres, have pine needles that are exceptionally long.

The newly-made roads through the forest have a good surface and are of sufficient width to park a car at the side. There are few signposts, so it is sensible to have a road map with you. The Pico de Tamadaba, 1,440 m, is a glorious summit that will appeal to lovers of nature, who will want to linger to enjoy the pure mountain air and peaceful isolation of the great forest.

Hikers and mountain climbers can continue on through the Barranco de Agaete to Los Berrazales and to the west coast. They will see countless rare plants in the crevices of the rocks and many wondrous views out across mountain peaks and uninhabited valleys below, before they finally reach sea level, near Agaete.

There is no easy road through the forest to the west coast so most tourists return by the same route, via Artenara to Cruz de Tejeda, thence to Las Palmas (but see also Inland route 5). Before completing the return trip a stop for refreshment may be made at the Parador Cruz de Tejeda, the state-run hotel and restaurant, whose entrance is close to the Cruz de Tejeda. Its bars and gardens open to non-residents, and the restaurant serves local dishes. There are also currency exchange facilities. The Canarian style building was designed by the architect Nestor de Torre. From the patio, on a clear day, a tremendous vista is obtained across the island and the seas to Tenerife and Gomera. Across the road from the Parador looking between the pine trees, it is sometimes possible to see Fuerteventura.

Inland route 4

(Pinar de Tamadaba — Cuevas de las Cruces: 40 kms; Pinar de Tamadaba — Mogan: 73 kms)

An extended tour by jeep or motorcycle via Artenara and Pinar de Tamadaba from Las Palmas or the south will be a thrilling experience for young holidaymakers. As many of the mountain roads are unmade and have tortuous bends, it is sensible either to travel in the company of an experienced driver or join one of the jeep tours that depart regularly from the main tourist centres: they are all well advertised in the local papers, most hotels and travel agents. Do allow plenty of time for the journey as the distance is deceptive.

If you are in a jeep and have a head for heights and a seat for bumpy rides, then it is possible to get from Tamadaba to the west coast by a minor road which goes past three manmade reservoirs, the so-called *presas,* to reach **Hoya de Pineda** — a beautiful but slow ride that leads down the mountains to just north of the **Cuevas de las Cruces** on the C810.

An even more adventurous route from the forest leads to Mogan on the southwest coast. This road is under construction and should only be taken on a fine day in a jeep, as the clouds can come down very quickly. The views are spectacular and well worth the inconvenience, and the silence is magical. We stress that this is a strenuous ride and should only be attempted by the really fit.

149

Inland route 5

(Cruz de Tejeda — Tejeda — San Bartolome de Tirajana — Fataga and Maspalomas: about 37 km: half day by car or taxi.)

Yet another way to return from the centre of the island, and more manageable for cars, is to turn south at Cruz de Tejeda towards the attractive village of **Tejeda.** Lying at over 914 m, it is pretty and peaceful with many orange and lemon groves. It has a useful petrol station. A twisting road passes craggy mountain peaks, including the Roque Bentayga, in a landscape reminiscent of the surface of the moon. At the village of **Ayacate** a quaint roadside bar is gaining much popularity.

The route descends very slowly from the mountains, alongside deep ravines so watch the unguarded sides to the road. Keep a look out for coaches and motorcaravans and be prepared to reverse in narrow places, sometimes with sheer edges! This exciting and pictorial drive will lead to **San Bartolome de Tirajana,** which is a veritable oasis at the foot of the crags. Palm trees abound and the land is terraced and cultivated, the red-roofed houses well built. It comes as quite a shock to return to civilisation after this drive in the remote and peaceful mountains.

From San Bartolome one can join the road to Aguimes, via Santa Lucia and Temisa — a distance of 23 kms though poor road conditions will make it seem much longer — enabling one to rejoin the C812 for the drive back to Las Palmas. Visitors who want to drive on to the south of the island can take the road via Fataga which leads down a long dry **barranco** to Maspalomas on the south coast. The tiny village of **Fataga** is being developed as a stopping place for coach excursions; several small shops have a selection of island crafts and ceramics for sale. In the bars, samples of local liqueurs are given freely. Try the Ron Miele Indias, a liqueur made of rum and honey; a bottle costs about 200 pesetas (£1) and it will taste wonderful after your mountain ride!

One further stop should be made along your route, at a viewpoint just south of **Arteara.** A splendid panorama shows the wonderous red ochre mountains, then the shoreline and modern hotels of Maspalomas, with the great sand dunes and the blue sea beyond.

The noise and bustle of the traffic as you reach Maspalomas contrasts sharply with the tranquillity of central Gran Canaria. Anyone who makes the journey from the north east coast through the Cumbre to the arid south cannot fail to appreciate the aptness of describing the island as 'a continent in miniature' for small as it is, there seems to be everything: fishing villages, an international port, old churches, green valleys, silent forests, ancient caves, craggy mountains, majestic peaks, historic sites and a desert-like zone. Together with modern comforts, entertainment and sports, and sea, sand and sunshine, these must put Gran Canaria very high on the list of beautiful islands.

8 Lanzarote

Isla del Fuego — Fire Island

Lanzarote is the lowest lying of the seven major Canary Islands, with a maximum height of 671 m at Penas del Chache in the Famara range of mountains. It is the fourth largest island, with an area of approximately 806 sq km and a population of 50,000. It is the most easterly of the Canary Islands, the closest to Africa, and also the most northerly of the main islands. Five smaller islands, Graciosa, Del Este, Alegranza, Montana Clara and Roques del Oeste belong to Lanzarote.

Three quarters of the island is covered with volcanic lava thrown up by a multitude of volcanoes during different periods. The volcanic zone of a past eruption which took place between 1730 and 1736, has now been designated the National Park of Timanfaya in the Montanas del Fuego (the Fire Mountains), so called because of the emanations of heat which are still present.

Because of its relative flatness, it seldom rains in Lanzarote and clouds are rare, except at times when the *sirocco* wind blows dust from the Sahara. Like most of the islands it has a range of mountains — here they run northeast to southwest — but because they are of no great height they do not attract much moisture. The coasts are mainly level, many have fine sandy beaches or rocky pools.

Lanzarote is said to be named after a Genoese sailor called Lancelotto who gained a foothold in the fourteenth century. Early Latin maps referred to the island as Insula de Lanzaotus, the Latin equivalent of the mariner's name.

The main impression of the island is of the contrasts between its natural and man-made beauty. The natural volcanic wonders are immensely impressive and vary considerably in different parts of the island, in places creating a lunar landscape quite incredible until seen. But equally notable is the way the inhabitants of this unusual country have clung to their land. With the passage of time, man seems to be able to adapt to the most unlikely of environments and the praiseworthy endeavours of the islanders of Lanzarote are as great an attraction as the wonders of nature.

The capital is Arrecife, a busy port with a fish-canning industry and a huge desalination plant which is the life blood of the island, turning the sea water into the much needed drinking water for daily use. Arrecife a sprawling town, and at this point of time rather a mess of re-building, but one is hopeful that given a few more years it will be as attractive as the rest of Lanzarote.

During the last twelve years tourism has progressed successfully: ocean-going cruise ships are able to dock, car and passenger ferries arrive regularly. A modern airport provides, via Las Palmas and Tenerife, a frequent service to UK and the rest of Europe. Most of the tourist complexes are in the south, where the best beaches are found, but other holiday areas are dotted towards the northern end of the island. Luxury hotels and apartments, restaurants and entertainments of international quality maintain a high standard.

Much credit for all this can be attributed to one man, César Manrique, born in Lanzarote in 1920, an artist and sculptor who has studied and worked all over the world. The love he has for his native land has inspired him to integrate tourism with, rather than impose upon it the vast wilderness of Lanzarote. As artistic consultant to the Cabildo (local government) he has produced outstanding modern designs which seem to achieve perfect harmony with the natural surroundings, and indeed, in places even enhance them. The fact that the islanders themselves appreciate his ideas and speak so highly of him, is significant. Lanzarote is amazingly clean and tidy, even the smallest villages have a neat appearance. Thanks to César Manrique, no large advertisements are displayed, no buildings, except in the capital Arrecife, can be more than four storeys high. Litter is not allowed on the beaches or in the streets. The local population takes immense pride in the 'ideal' situation which is being created.

Despite the lack of rainfall and poor agricultural soil, the people of Lanzarote contrive to produce onions, tomatoes and potatoes for export. Also grown are melons, peas, beans, lentils, chickpeas and maize. The wine of the island (*Malvasia*) is good, rather like a dry sherry, and can be 17° proof. Sufficient is produced for it to be exported.

Practically none of the cultivation is irrigated, so it must rely on what rainfall and moisture there is. The people have overcome this difficulty covering the soil with black volcanic ash to a depth of about ten to fifteen centimetres. The ash stops evaporation and also absorbs the early morning dew, which

153

provides moisture for the underlying soil. The soil and ash have to be replaced every twenty to thirty years. All round the island the pattern of the landscape is black ash, small volcanic humps and oases of neat white modern buildings, with green palm trees making a graceful contrast to the sharper outlines.

Fishing helps the Lanzarote economy. The fleet operates mainly off the neighbouring coast of North Africa. Large salt pans at Janubio produce about 10,000 tons annually and most of it is used in the conservation of fish, though it is also refined and used for kitchen and table salt.

Tenerife and Gran Canaria were, until recently, the only islands with full holiday facilities. Now Lanzarote is in third place and fast developing. It aims to attract a discerning public and holidaymakers will find a harmonious island, full of comfort and spectacular attractions. The island provides varied opportunities for water sports: deep sea fishing, yacht sailing and wind surfing; skuba diving in the clear waters, which contain a variety of underwater marine life. It is on record that no dangerous fish such as shark, have been seen close to the shores.

Climate

Lanzarote is similar to the other Canary Islands, with spring like weather all year round. The absence of any large central mountain means the difference in temperature between the north and the south is minimal. In summer the maximum temperature is 25°C an in winter the average is 17°C.

Clothes

Lightweight clothes are worn all year round. A windproof jacket or cardigan for windy days or a rare cool evening may be required. Bikinis are worn only on the beach. In hotels it is useful to have a robe to wear over swim clothes, when going for a dip in the pool. Casual or trendy clothes are worn in the evening. It is not necessary to wear full evening dress.

The growing popularity of nudism has led to the establishment of a centre for enthusiasts at Charco de Palo Club at **Castillo de Papagayo** in Mala (Haria). Another is under construction at Guatiza.

Getting about

Lanzarote's tarmac roads are very good and on them travel is no problem but a few unmade country roads will need more care, as they are little more than rough tracks and may have potholes.

Buses run to all the main places, the routes being to the north, central and south. Buses are state controlled and resonably priced. Timetables can be obtained at the Tourist Office or Bus Office, Transportes Lanzarote SA at Garcia Escames 71, Arrecife. Example of price: Arrecife to Playa Blanca, in the extreme south, is 145 pesetas (74p).

Taxis are much in evidence; there is a tariff of fixed charges, which averages at 200 pesetas (£1) for five kilometres. Always confirm your price before your journey. Excursions by taxi, touring the island can be made from Hotel Fariones, Puerto del Carmen. A southern route, taking about four hours and covering 90 kilometres, would cost about 3000 pesetas (£15).

Coach Tours

Tours of the island are run by several *Viajes,* (travel agents) including Ultramar Express SA, Centro Commercial, La Penita, Puerto del Carmen. Three main tours cover most of the tourist routes.

The northern route goes from Arrecife through the agricultural area of the north, to the famed look-out point Mirador del Rio. A visit is made to two different volcanic caves of much interest, plus a stop at a *bodega* for an opportunity to taste and purchase some of the local Malvasia wine.

The central and southern route goes into the area which is all black lava sand and small villages. The white flat-topped houses, with their green doors contrast strongly. The drive goes past salt works and then visits the Timanfaya National Park and up to the Fire Mountain. An opportunity is given to ride a camel, an experience that should be made at least once in a lifetime!

The third tour covers the beaches of the south, with the tourist areas of Los Pocillos, Puerto del Carmen, then further south to Playa Blanca and Papagayo.

These tours take a minimum of four hours but often are extended to a full-day tour, which includes lunch in a restaurant. Prices average from 1,500 pesetas (£8) to 2,000 pesetas (£10) each tour.

Car hire

Self-drive cars are being used increasingly by holidaymakers, and all the main tourist places, including Arrecife, have car-hire firms. A Seat Panda 127, which takes five persons, costs 1,500 pesetas (£8) a day, plus insurance of 350 pesetas (£2) and a 2% tax. Petrol is not included. It should be noted that petrol stations are closed on Sundays and Public Holidays.

Shopping

Lanzarote is an island with an abundance of supermarkets. Even in the smallest village you will find the little self-service store with trolleys and baskets. Goods are priced and a large range of commodities is available. Prices are slightly higher than in Tenerife or Gran Canaria, no doubt due to the extra cost of transportation.

Handicraft shops are to be found in all the tourist centres. Hand embroidery, local pottery, costume rag dolls are much in evidence. Big straw hats, as worn by the workers in the fields and palm woven boxes are on sale. The *Timple,* a handmade stringed instrument, manufactured in Teguise at the workshop of Juan Morales, is an unusual purchase. Jewellery and ornaments fashioned from Olivin (peridot), the semi precious green stone found in the lava rock are pretty and something different to seek.

History

Lanzarote and the adjacent isles, including Fuerteventura, were long ago known as the *Purpurarias,* after the Orchilla, which was collected to make a purple dye. The original inhabitants were the Guanches, thought to be of North African origin. The first real European foothold here was secured by the Genoese in the fourteenth century but it was finally taken over by the French invader, Jean de Bethencourt, in the fifteenth century, under orders from Spain. Since then Lanzarote has belonged to Spain.

However the island was subsequently the victim of many pirate raids. The Portuguese, Diego de Silva attacked the island in 1459 but he tempered his aggression and married a daughter of the Lord of Lanzarote, Diego García de Herrea. The famous Frenchman known as 'Peg Leg', ransacked Arrecife and Arals Calafat landed in 1569 and took some two hundred slaves. In 1617, even the British under Sir Walter Raleigh, carried out a raid. A year later the Algerians, Tabac and Soliman, with over thirty ships, landed and took almost a thousand prisoners. The people of Lanzarote had constantly to take refuge in fortresses or to hide in caves.

With the eruption of the volcano, Timanfaya, in 1730 came an even worse disaster, for eruptions continued for six years, destroying over a quarter of the island with lava and ash. Only the stoic tenacity of the inhabitants enabled them to survive. Despite the *Malpais* (literally 'bad lands') of volcanic waste, the inhabitants toiled at fishing and agriculture, using donkeys and camels plus human endeavour, to create a way of life.

Today, with half the population living in Arrecife, tourism is being developed into a major industry. With its wonderful climate and the friendly nature of its inhabitants, its large range of facilities, beaches, sport and leisure centres, and some amazing natural wonders, Lanzarote must surely be one of the most 'original' of holiday destinations.

Arrecife, the capital

Arrecife, the port and capital of Lanzarote, with a population of about 30,000, is in the throes of modernisation to cope with the increase of tourist traffic. A system of one-way streets seems to confuse rather than assist the traffic flow. Most roads are narrow and pedestrians walk in the streets where parked cars obstruct. However it is, on the whole, an easy-going place; the frantic blowing of whistles by policemen as tourists commit minor traffic errors is met with good humour from the townsfolk.

Arriving at **Arrecife,** the port and capital of Lanzarote, by sea, one looks upon an island of 'brown pimples' small volcanic mountains dotted all along the dry brown landscape. Puerto de los Marmoles is at the eastern edge of Arrecife.

City tour 1

(Castillo de San José: 15 minute drive)

Driving out of the port towards the town, there is a large Cepsa petrol station on the south side of the road. At the side of this petrol station is a road, which has no name at present, leading towards the Castillo de San José, an eighteenth century fortress which has recently been restored. Open from 1100 to 2100 hrs, admission free.) Inside is found an International Contemporary Art Museum, created by César Manrique. The design is so modern that it is hard to remember that one is really in an ancient fort. Downstairs, a smart high-class restaurant has huge windows giving a clear picture of the harbour below. The restaurant is one of the more expensive on the island, luxuriously laid out with black leather bar and modern sculpture. The toilets are worth a special mention, as they have been made into a veritable garden grotto with trailing plants everywhere! Outside the paved patio and carpark afford good views of ships and the harbour which are floodlit at night.

Along the main road (Carreterra de los Marmoles), leading into Arrecife there are factories and the most untidy scrubland in all Lanzarote. A ring road allows you to bypass Arrecife if you have no need to visit it.

City tour 2

(Castillo de San Gabriel — Market — Iglesia de San Gines: 3 hour walk)

The original large natural harbour in front of the town is protected by a series of little islets. One, the Islote de los Ingléses is connected by an old drawbridge to the **Castillo de San Gabriel.** Torrani, an Italian architect in the reign of Philip II of Spain, built this sturdy fortress to defend the port from pirates. Two well-preserved old cannons stand outside as a reminder of past aggressive history. Inside the castle is housed the Archeology Museum, full of ancient fossils, sub aqua finds and Guanche relics. Open daily from 0900 to 1300 and 1500 to 1800 hrs, except Sundays and public holidays. Admission is 50 pesetas (25 pence).

The waterfront from the drawbridge southwards has a pleasant promenade with seats, statues, beds of flowers and colourful pergolas. It is along this promenade the **Tourist Office**

158

of Lanzarote (Officina de Turismo), is situated in the Parque Municipal de Arrecife. This is on the sea side of the road, in a low Canarian type building; at present there is no sign outside to indicate that it is the Tourist Office! An English-speaking lady inside will be helpful. Visitors to Lanzarote can use the services of professional guides and interpreters; a guided tour of the south would cost 3,400 pesetas (£17).

Halfway along the seafront on the inland side, in a street called Calle Liebre, you will find the **market.** It seems very small compared with the one in Tenerife, but has daily supplies of fruit and vegetables, some imported. Locally grown onions, potatoes, tomatoes, melons and delicious green peas are reasonably priced. Fresh white goats' cheese is of excellent quality and makes a sustaining mid-day lunch. A small amount of fresh pork is sold in the market. A *Carniceria* (butcher) selling a full range of meats and sausages is to be found in the main part of the town. In a separate building is a fresh fish market which has a plentiful selection.

Arrecife has several fish packing factories, especially for sardines and tuna. This, apart from tourism, is the island's major industry.

The main street along the front is called Generalisimo Franco, post office (*correos*) is situated here, open from 0900 to 1300 and 1600 to 1900 hrs, except Saturday afternoon and Sunday. The busiest street is the Leon Y Castillo, with one-way traffic, north from the seafront. Banks are to be found there, opening 0900 to 1300 hrs.

The principal church, **Iglesia de san Gines,** eighteenth century, is dedicated to the island's patron saint. Small gift shops sell an assortment of tourist souvenirs, but a wider selection can be obtained in the larger tourist complexes of the south. Most everyday commodities are available but Arrecife is not a town for a large spending-spree.

Arrecife has one four-star hotel and two that are three-star, plus two one-star guesthouses. Arrecife Gran Hotel, at the southern end of the promenade, Avenida de la Mancomunidad, is the tallest building in the town and stands out prominently on the skyline. With 154 well appointed bedrooms and two suites with terrace facing the sea, it is comfortable and quiet. Outside is a sun patio and a swimming pool with toilets and showers nearby; children have their own pool. Sauna, gymnasium, tennis courts, table tennis and children's playground are all right by the sea. This hotel is excellent for anyone who likes to be in the town.

There are several pleasant bars and restaurants in Arrecife. One of the easiest places to find is the Cafeteria Avenida in the Avenida Mancomunidad, one of a row of cafés on the main promenade. You can sit on the terrace and watch the passing scene, enjoying coffee or a sandwich, even steak and chips. For a quieter ambience seek out Marisqueria Abdon, 54 Calle Canelejas, just behind Cafeteria Avenida. This is an owner-run restaurant with a high reputation.

A good *à la carte* menu is international and written in English. The *menu del dia* (menu of the day) costs 510 pesetas (£2.60) and will consist of soup, main course (usually excellent fresh fish) sweet, bread and a quarter litre of wine included in the price. Sea foods are much in demand, and you can select your own fish from those swimming in a glass tank. Do not go to the restaurant too early if you wish to have the company of the local people, who usually start their midday meal at about 1400 hrs.

Few dishes originate in Lanzarote but it is worth ordering a local dish where the fish called *vieja* is cooked whole in a deep pan and seasoned with potatoes, oil and vinegar. The juices are served first as a soup. Fried kid (young goat) and *papas arrugadas* (little new potatoes cooked in seawater) are very popular. At Christmas time a speciality is *truchas,* a dessert made from sweet potato paste.

Night life in Arrecife is limited, There is a cinema which shows mainly Spanish films or films dubbed in Spanish. The Bambi Night Club, behind the Cafe de Paris, is on Avenida Mancomunidad almost opposite the Arrecife Gran Hotel. Open 2000 to 0300 hrs. This is mainly disco music and sometimes a group is featured. For the 'redlight' district take the Arrecife to Tahice road at the poorer end of town.

Island tour 1 — south

(Arrecife — Aeropuerto de Lanzarote — Playa de Pocillos —
Puerto del Carmen — Playa Blanca: about 19 km; half-day tour
by car, taxi or bus)

The GC720 road out of Arrecife goes west past an *urbanizaćion*
of modern villas, **Playa Honda**, where the wealthy of Arrecife
have their new modern homes. Six kilometres further on is the
turn-off for the **Aeropuerto de Lanzarote.** Those arriving by air
in Lanzarote have a delightful surprise when they reach the
airport building; even the most blasé traveller could not fail to
be impressed by its unique decor and sheer cleanliness. Again
it is the hand of Cesar Manrique which guided the creation of
this superb airport lounge. Supported on plain white pillars is a
green and white striped canvas awning that stretches the entire
area of the roof, so that the effect is like being in a cool tent.
Grouped round the pillars on the smoothly tiled floor are attractive green and white low cushioned seats and tables. Let into the
ceiling are areas of light under which banks of tropical ferns are
placed. So the scene is set to prepare visitors for the unique
quality of the island of Lanzarote.

Two kilometres further south from the airport turning, the
main road continues towards Tias and Yaiza. Taking the left-
hand turn towards the coast, the road leads to a large, flat sandy
bay called **Playa de los Pocillos,** and the start of the modern
resorts. Well developed with plenty of open spaces, clear
water, clean beaches, and the near certainty of warm sunshine,
this locality is a delightful haven for holidaymakers.

For those seeking hotel accommodation, the four-star Hotel
San Antonio will provide a warm welcome. Opened in
December 1972, it has 331 well-maintained bedrooms, all with
sea view and balcony, air conditioning, radio, private bethroom
and comfortable beds. It has a restaurant, two bars, night club,
discotheque, snack bar, shops and large children's playroom.
Outside large terraces and patios and a heated seawater
swimming pool are set in decorative gardens. Plenty of layout
chairs and bathing towels are provided free. As the hotel is
right at the edge of the beach you can also enjoy the sands or
rocky beach pools. To combat the scarcity of water and electricity the hotel has installed its own desalination plant and
generators, also a sewage plant. The hotel is British-owned and
used by several British tour operators. The director of the hotel
is Canarian and speaks English.

Opposite this hotel a complex of shops, bars, cafes, restaurant and travel agents provide for a variety of requirements. Nearby villa and apartment accommodation is pleasantly laid out, within easy reach of everything.

Just a short walk from the Playa de los Pocillos, along the coast, the road leads into **Playa Blanca,** usually referred to as **Puerto del Carmen** (the small port is at the far end). Again this mecca for holidaymakers has a large hotel, the four-star Los Fariones, set close to the sea and providing luxury comforts. Villas and apartments, often with their own swimming pools, gardens full of colour and tropical palms seem to meet every requirement. Numerous shopping arcades, eating establishments, car hire firms and facilities for various sports activities create a relaxed and easy going atmosphere.

Establishments with names like the Bristol Bar, The Victorian Inn with English draught beer, La Pizza, Restaurant Chino, Cafe Cristina, the Bierkeller indicate what you may expect from them in the way of food and drink. Midday meals are priced around 400 pesetas (£2.04), evening menus start at 500 pesetas (£2.56). Night clubs, including the Tahiche Club, attached to the Fariones Hotel, are open from 2200 to 0200 hrs, admission is free and on Friday nights there is folk dancing.

At the western end of Puerto del Carmen, a small harbour wall is all that remains of the original fishing port, tourism having taken over completely these days. The road that leads north away from the sea and out of town, Calle Juan Carlos 1, is lined with shops which serve the nearby holiday villas. Banks in Puerto del Carmen are open from 0900 to 1300 and 1600 to 1800 hrs.

Island tour 2 — south

(Playa Blanca — Tias — Yaiza — Salinas de Janubio — El Golfo — Playa Blanca Sud — Punta Papagayo: about 67 km; half day by car or taxi)

From the main highway, GC720, the route continues southwest through **Tias,** a small town of Canarian inhabitants but no special tourist attractions. The road winds its way through low volcanic mountains, dry and bar of natural vegetation. A curious agricultural system known as *Macetas* (flowerpots) is used. Deep holes are dug in the earth and protected by lava stones; the hole is then partially covered with fine black granules of lava *picon*, which are moisture retaining. Amongst the crops planted in *macetas* are tomatoes, onions, and grapes for the wine known as *Malvasia.* This form of agriculture is unique to Lanzarote.

The village of **Uga** sits in a little depression of land. White-washed houses and palm trees give it an air of peacefulness. A restaurant and bar, called the Timanfaya, is a low rambling house with vine covered patio and an outside barbecue. It is sometimes used by coach parties at midday and during the evening; on special occasions folk dancing and music are organized.

Two kilometres along the main road, (GC720) one reaches the town of **Yaiza,** sometimes called the capital of the south. It is reminiscent of North Africa with its low flat-topped white houses and tall palm trees. The spotlessly clean and attractive appearance of Yaiza has earned it awards from the local government and praise for its inhabitants. The central square creates a splendid setting for the large white eighteenth-century church of Los Remidos. Built in 1785, it high belltower stands out strikingly against the clear blue sky. In the square in front of the church decorative lampstands have cacti and bright flowers banked around them, and seats are positioned beneath huge trees for a shady rest.

Walking around this tidy little village is a delight, especially if you are fortunate enough to be there at the quieter moments. It is interesting to note how the villagers accept the hordes of foreigners who peer and stare into every nook and cranny, their cameras always alert for an intimate photograph. These same tourists can enjoy a very good meal at the Restaurant el Volcan. The 'menu of the day' costs 575 pesetas (£3). Soup, freshly cooked fish, salad, potatoes, fruit and ice cream, plus bread and wine make a tasty good-value meal and service is prompt and all is clean and friendly. Leaving the cool atmosphere of the restaurant you will probably reach for your sunglasses when you go out into the brilliant sunshine!

A long-established restaurant in the village is La Era, in an old farmhouse built around a courtyard with grain stores and stables serving as dining rooms. It has been decorated with ferns and ceramics and candlelight enhances the picture, while the air is fragrant with mimosa and other sweet smelling plants. An 'a la carte' menu offers a good choice; allow about 1000 pesetas (£5) per person.

Villages in Lanzarote have low, flat topped, whitewashed houses with green doors. They make a striking contrast to the surrounding fields and small mountains of black lava ash.

Continuing westwards beyond Yaiza, one enters a flat area of volcanic *malpais* (bad lands). Except at a spot two kilometres out of Yaiza, where a tourist shop and bar restaurant has recently been built there is total wilderness on both sides of road. Used specially by coach parties, the shop has a good selection of local hand-made gifts so it is a convenient place for souvenir shopping.

As a backcloth to the terrible wasteland, the Fire Mountain, **Timanfaya,** and the volcanic peaks of the National Park can be seen: huge red bronze coloured peaks, deep crevices making dark shadows, the lines and depressions still showing where the lava and earth has been torn asunder.

Six kilometres on from Yaiza the road goes past a large coastal sea lake, the **Salinas de Janubio.** The lake is harvested for salt and has an annual production of 10,000 tons. There is a road down to the entrance where you can view the various processes. To obtain the salt, seawater is pumped into square 'pans', areas where the natural evaporation by sun and wind dries out the moisture. The pumping used formerly to be done by a windmill. After about four weeks the salt is removed and put into piles to dry. The white pyramid shapes of salt make a very unusual picture, as the lake often has a turquoise blue appearance. It is interesting to know that some of the salt is used for the festival of Corpus Cristi, every spring, when the local artists dye the salt various colours, then use it to create religious pictures in the streets of Arrecife.

The lake area is a haunt of migrant birds and resident water-fowl so it is popular with ornithologists.

Continuing on the coastal road, the drive becomes really spectacular, with twists and turns along a shallow clifftop of lava rocks. There are some breathtaking views of erroded lava which juts out to sea, forming amazing holes and caverns where the Atlantic rollers pound the sea into cascades of swirling foam. The sunlight glints and glistens in a rainbow of colour, as wave upon wave crash against the weird shapes, water spilling and splashing in endless motion. At **Los Hervideros** (Bubbling Spring) steps have been made across the lava rocks so that tourists may clamber down to nearly sea level, to get really close to the gushing waters inside the caves — a fascinating spectacle.

Finally one reaches the end of the road, where a large carpark is situated under a huge rock face. From here it is a short walk to visit one of the great wonders of Lanzarote **El Golfo.**

This was a volcano formed in contact with the sea which produced some rare and beautiful stratifications of different colours and shapes. A lagoon has been formed inside the crater by the infilteration of seawater. Because of microscopic organisms and its unfathomable depth, the lagoon water is bright emerald green, a most unusual sight, making one look twice to believe the colour is not manmade.

All this is set at beach level, so it makes a good place for a picnic. The beach is of pebbles but there are some flat rocky areas. At low tide there is a good view of a natural platform of rock that lies just offshore, looking like a perfect auditorium for performances by mermaids!

From Salinas de Janiubio a good road goes down to the southern tip of Lanzarote, to a place called **Playa Blanca**, not to be confused with the Playa Blanca near Puerto del Carmen. This Playa Blanca is a small fishing port and resort close to some of the island's best beaches, in the area of El Rubicon where Bethencourt established his first settlement. All that remains is an old tower at the cliff edge.

It is from the Puerto at Playa Blanca that a car ferry operates, three times daily, to Coralejo in Fuerteventura, (weather permitting — for the seas can be very rough in that small channel). The journey takes thirty minutes, tickets are available at both ports and at travel agents. Fishing boats and yachts also use the harbour at Playa Blanca, which is being developed for tourists. Already there are a number of villas and an *urbanización* of time-sharing apartments, but it still retains the quiet fishing village feeling.

The village has two good supermarkets, and look for the pleasant fish restaurants by the sea. A pretty esplanade along the seafront adjoins the small sandy beach. A simple, clean two star hostel has eight rooms; a double room costs 1,400 pesetas (£2.06).

To reach **Papagayo Punta** the southernmost tip of the island, it is necessary to travel on a rough dirt track road for a distance of four kilometres or so. No doubt this road will be improved in time, but at the moment it is a feat of endurance, bumping over the uneven surface across rocky sandy dunes. However on arrival there is a feeling that it was worth the effort. Clean golden sands lead to clear calm seas and ideal swimming. Walks can be made along the headland, where a climb down to rocky creeks and sandy coves provides access to perfect (though unofficial!) naturist beaches.

Salt flats at Janubio are seen in various stages of drying with piles of salt cooking like miniature white pyramids. The salt is also used every spring for the Corpus Christi festival when it is dyed various colours and used to create wonderful religious pictures in the streets of Arrecife.

One of nature's weird sights can be seen at El Golfo, where the inner rim of a volcano is open for all to wonder at the various coloured rock strata which extend into the sea.

Island tour 3

(Timanfaya National Park: about 3 hours)

Timanfaya National Park, situated in the western part of Lanzarote, five kilometres north of Yaiza, must be one of the most extraordinary national parks in the world. Because of the special characteristics of the spectacles to be seen here, and of the geology of the park visitors are requested to abide by the rules for its use and to follow the instructions of the official guides. The most spectacular and interesting zone of the eruption can be visited by way of the Volcanic Route: there are periodic departures from Islote de Hilario, a restaurant and view-point.

The present area of the park is about 200 sq kms. The range of **Montanas del Fuego de Timanfaya** emerged during the great eruptions of 1730 which lasted for six years. This tremendous volcanic activity transformed the physical characteristics of the south of the island, where thirty-two new craters were formed in the midst of a sea of lava and cinders.

This event, considered to be one of the most important in volcanology, had an exceptional eye witness. The priest of the nearby village of Yaiza, Don Andres Lorenzo Curbelo, wrote in his diary the most significant details. He describes the beginning of the eruption as follows, "On the first day of September, between nine and ten at night, the earth suddenly opened up near Timanfaya, two leagues from Yaiza and an enormous mountain rose from the bosom of the earth, and from its apex shot flames which continued to burn for nineteen days." The eruptions were to continue and destroy whole villages and farmlands for another six years.

Sometimes red, sometimes black, this vast lunar landscape now has roads across it. A toll of 150 pesetas (77p) is charged at the entrance. Visiting hours are from 0900 to 1700 hrs.

The road twists and winds through jagged lava rocks, sinister and black, through a sea of desolation, grim and weird yet with a tremendous grandeur that seems unreal.

The Islote de Hilario is a circular restaurant and bar, built out of lava stone which blends unobtrusively with the landscape. It is built on the site of a hut which belonged to an old hermit, Hilario, who (it is said) returned with his donkey after the devastation and planted a fig tree, the only vegetation in the area and an ancestor of the one now growing in the middle of the restaurant.

The volcanoes may be quiescent but their inner fires still burn and bubble. At Islote de Hilario impressive demonstrations are given of this phenomenon. Twigs of the ulaga bush are dropped into a hole in the ground only 50 centimetres deep: they smoulder and then catch fire. Water is poured into a pipe in the lava, and it evaporates immediately and shoots out as a spectacular burst of steam. Ashes scooped up in a shovel, when held in the hand become uncomfortably hot. Food in the restaurant is cooked over a specially prepared hole in the ground, a natural charcoal grill. Have a meal cooked by a volcano!

From Islote de Hilario tourists can take an hour's bus ride with a taped commentary and music, through the lava to the top of the crater of Timanfaya to get an idea what the surface of the moon is like. It is a fact that the first astronauts were shown photographs of the National Park of Timanfaya to prepare them for their expedition.

For the more ardent travellers, there are camel rides up the side of the volcanic mountain (about 400 pesetas (£2.06)) two people sit on either side of a dromedary (always referred to as a camel) in specially constructed wooden chairs. The camels jerk and jog their way slowly to the top of the volcano, their flat feet plodding carefully over the loose ashes. Passengers are not strapped into the chairs, so a sense of balance and strength is required to enjoy the moment! Watch out for the sudden jerk forward as the huge beast gets up off its knees. Once on the move, it is an exhilarating feeling, provided you do not mind the sight of a camel's muzzled mouth coming alongside you from behind, its yellow teeth looking dangerously evil. It seems that no one has ever been known to fall off his camel on one of these trips, and practically everyone has a hilarious time. Suspended over the side of a camel on the black cinder slopes of the volcano, with the warm sunshine and blue skies above, somehow seems an appropriately unusual way of appreciating the strange attractions of this mysterious landscape with its dark red cones in their silent majesty motionless and fearfully beautiful.

The camels are imported from North Africa when three years old and live for about twenty five years. They are used for ploughing, often harnessed with a donkey — an odd mixture, but it seems that these creatures are compatible.

One of the most amazing sights in Lanzarote is to be on the Fire Mountain when one of the guides pours into a hole in the ground, a small amount of water. This immediately turns into a fierce jet of steam and you realize that the name Fire Mountain is no joke and that one is really standing on thermal ground.

Island tour 4 — central

(Timanfaya — Mancha Blanca — Tinajo — Tiagua — Mozaga — San Bartolomé — Arrecife: about 30 km; half day by car or taxi:)

To the east and north of the Timanfaya National Park, in the part known as **La Geria,** the landscape is less harsh but equally novel. This is a comparatively high productive area where vines are grown in little man-made craters of black ash, called *picon*, often sheltered from the winds by low semi-circular stone walls. It is a sight not easily forgotten.

The main road north from Timanfaya passes through **Mancha Blanca** where, so the legend tells us, Our Lady of the Sorrows appeared and commanded the flow of molten lava to stop, thus saving the village from being destroyed. A church was built in village; it is now the hermitage of Nuestra Señora de los Volcanes, and the scene of an important fiesta each year on 15th September.

Around **Tinajo** tobacco and tomatoes are grown and some green areas are to be seen amongst small farms and villages. The main road goes east and then south through **Tiagura** and on to **Mozaga** which is in the centre of the island. Situated at the side of the crossroads is a notable monument, La Fecundidad, a statue created in metal by César Manrique, to honour the courage of the peasants of Lanzarote. It is 15 m high and ultra-modern, contrasting sharply with the scenery. What used to be a humble cottage nearby, has now been transformed into a museum and restaurant: El Monumento has a courtyard with a *bodega* where you can taste the country wines. In the restaurant, try the local stew, *Puchero* — braised goat's meat served with *gofio* balls. These are rather like dumplings, rolled in a piece of goatskin for shaping before being fried and dunked in stew.

Another interesting feature of the area around **San Bartolomé,** the next township, are the crops which are protected by low straw windbreaks. The ingenuity of the country people of Lanzarote is quite amazing. San Bartolomé is the country town that boasts its own folk group, called Ajey, which has been very successful in national and international competitions.

The road from San Bartolomé now leads you back to Arrecife at the end of the tour of the centre of the island.

Island tour 5 — north

(Arrecife — Tahice — Teguise — La Caleta — Haria — Mirador del Rio: about 78 km; half day by car or taxi)

The route for this northern tour of the island starts from Arrecife and runs first through the small village of **Tahice,** now renowned as the home of the island's beloved César Manrique His uniquely designed modern house, built deep into the lava rock, has been featured on international television, but is not open to the public.

César Manrique, born in 1920, has become an artist and sculptor of international fame. In 1968 he returned to live in Lanzarote, and since then he has done much to enhance and enrich the natural beauty of his homeland. Often strikingly modern and unusual, his work has a pure simplicity of line and he makes use of natural stones, objects and materials, to blend harmoniously with the spirit of modern Lanzarote.

Passing **Nazaret,** a small village of low flat-topped houses, the road leads to **Teguise,** one of the oldest towns in the Canary Islands and formerly the capital of Lanzarote. In a peaceful square is the Palace of Spinola, a beautiful sixteenth century mansion, now restored and open to the public. Across from the Palace is the huge church of San Miguel looking like a fortress; the original building was sacked and ruined on several occasions by pirates. Among other buildings of historic interest are the Convents of Santo Domingo and San Francisco, recently renovated. It is in Teguise that local craftsmen manufacture the *timple,* a small guitar-like instrument used for all folklore music in the Islands.

On the summit of the nearby volcano of **Guanapay,** stands the castle of Santa Barbara, the oldest fort on the island. Originally a sixteenth century watch tower against the Moors, it was extended following the attack by the French pirate Francisco el Clerigo. From the castle there are fine panoramic views across the island, even to Fuerteventura on a clear day.

A detour can be made from Teguise to the coast by leaving Teguise on the road for Mozaga and, at 4 km, taking the right turning towards the coast where there is the small fishing village of **La Caleta** and, to the right of the bay, **Playa Famara.** A modern *urbanización* set below a large cliff has the use of the sandy beach. In the village little has been done to destroy its native simplicity. Several simple bar-restaurants provide inexpensive meals in local surroundings. At the western end of the village an unspoilt beach of sand dunes and rocks, remains little frequented and a small development at the extreme end has not spoiled the tranquillity.

Returning to Teguise and following the road signposted Haria towards the northern tip of the island, one reaches the agricultural area of **Los Valles,** sometimes called the Valley of the Ten Thousand Palms. Scattered homesteads and dwellings give the countryside a very peaceful air. It is interesting to see that in some places because of lack of rich soil the vines are grafted into the rootstock of the prickly pear, a moisture retaining plant.

Los Valles is noteworthy because it is here that the people from the south, whose villages were destroyed by the Timanfaya volcanic eruption, were resettled. Their tenacity in struggling against the elements of fire and water to recreate a form of agriculture and way of life against all odds, is an admirable example of man's love for his homeland.

The road to **Haria** winds in a mountainous spiral. At the summit it is surprising to find that the land continues to be terraced and cultivated. Young onions are growing in neatly laid out rows. Maybe you will see the seedlings being planted by hand — a laborious task. No wonder that the farmer may stop to stare and at the same time eat a few of the onion seedlings! The geometrical patterns made by these tidy fields are a noticeable feature of the island.

Two bar-restaurants have been recently built on separate belvederes, affording splendid views northwards overlooking the valley below and the town of Haria, set amid many palm trees. The bars are used by coach tours, and they make a useful parking place, having toilets and small souvenir shops. Haria, amid some of the most fertile fields in Lanzarote, has a picturesque setting. Wild flowers and grass grow along the valley roads and neat white houses, bright with geraniums, bougainvillea, palm and eucalyptus trees, make a colourful picture.

Approaching the extreme north tip of the island, the land again becomes bare and dry with only the odd cactus and cardon growing. It is worth remembering that cacti have very small needles that can cause much discomfort under the skin. Likewise the candelabra-like cardon (a tall spliky column cactus) if broken will give a copius discharge of milk sap which is very sticky, so protect your eyes and clothes.

A tall headland, the **Riscos de Famara,** stands out proudly, the basaltic rocks having sharp points. This site was the Bateria del Rio (battery) built in the sixteenth century, as a defence against pirate ships. Today a cleverly designed restaurant and glassed in look-out point built into the rockface enables visitors to enjoy an outstanding panoramic view. The Mirador del Rio is another of César Manrique's inspired tourist attractions. Admission 40 pesetas (20p). Open from 1100 to 1900 hrs.

The exterior of the restaurant is entirely covered with lava rock, but inside all is white and green (the Lanzarote motif colours) with white-washed walls, and enormous baskets of *elechos* (ferns) hanging down in cascades of cool green. A narrow balcony just a couple of metres wide, on the far side of the restaurant, allows anyone with a good head for heights to stand right at the edge of a precipice. Down below is the narrow channel of sea called **El Rio,** which flows between Lanzarote and Isla Graciosa. Most days the smaller islands of Roque del Oste, Roque del Este, Montana Clara and Alegranza can be clearly seen. On the beach some salt pans have a strange red glow, while across the water on Graciosa the pure white sands beckon invitingly.

At the bar in the Mirador there is a good selection of drinks and *tappas*. Try some *queso blanco* (goat's cheese) with a glass of cool white wine, then perhaps a portion of delicious creamy gateaux decorated with chocolate or fruits. Upstairs above the bar is a small shop selling a few local handicrafts. In the true Manrique style of not being flamboyant there is no sign to show you the way, you have to seek it out!

Island tour 6 — north

(Mirador del Rio — Orzola — Cueva de los Verdes — Grotto
Jameos del Agua — Arrieta — Mala — Guatiza — Costa Teguise
— Playa de los Charcos — Arrecife: about 46 km; half day by
car or taxi)

Now the road turns southwards, passing the village of **Ye,** the
road is signposted to the Cueva de los Verdes and Jameos del
Agua. Six kilometres from the Mirador del Rio, a turning left
goes to **Orzola,** a tiny port on the coast. This quiet fishing
village off the main tourist route has a beach and several bars.
Bar Restaurant el Callao and Restaurant los Roques both serve
excellent fish meals at reasonable prices.

From Orzola it is sometimes possible to take a boat over to the
island of La Graciosa. This has to be arranged through a travel
agent or at Orzola. The cost is 600 pesetas (£3.10) return but
the trip depends very much on the weather and the inclination
of the local fishermen. La Graciosa (42 sq km) has a population
of 800, who all live in the village of **Caleta del Sebo.** There are
some lovely bathing beaches there, and talk of further development for tourists. The other small islands are uninhabited.

Cueva de los Verdes is in an area of ancient volcanic activity,
twelve kilometres south of the Mirador del Rio. Again due to
Manrique's dislike of blatant signs, you will have to look hard
for the entrance to the caves, for very little is seen from above
the ground. Look for a sign showing the 'devil of Timanfaya' —
a weird face carved on a piece of pinewood. Thousands of years
ago during the Corona volcano eruption, a stream of molten lava
solidified into a tunnel, the lava outside cooling more quickly
than the central flow, thus creating these caves that were used
by the Guanches as a refuge from marauding pirates. Today
there is a series of caves six kilometres long, with several more
galleries not yet fully opened. Some are under the sea and are
of great geological interest. Guided tours and coach parties are
shown some of the wonders of these subterranean passages.
Open from 1100 to 1800 hrs, admission 110 pesetas (57p). The
visit takes about an hour, and it is an eerie experience to go
single file along these dimly lit and often narrow passages; in
places it is necessary to stoop low to pass into a larger cavern.
At one place called El Refugio (where the Guanches lived) a
small auditorium has been created, and concealed lighting used
to good effect. Remember to wear flat shoes and to put on dark
glasses as you come out of the cave, for the glare of the sunshine can be blinding — and mind your head!

Not far away, nearer the sea, in another part of the caves network created by the Corona eruption, is the **Grotto Jameos del Agua,** a natural phenomenon and now one of Lanzarote's main tourist attractions. The combined forces of nature and the clever, loving hand of mankind have achieved a fairylike 'Alladin's Cave'. Down a short flight of winding steps is a grotto, the sides of which are still in their natural state. Using lava stones a bar has been built: wooden tables and chairs are set amid huge cactus plants and hanging ferns while bright flowers add colour and softness, and subdued lighting gives depth.

Walking further into the cavern and down more steps, one reaches the floor of the cave where there is a shallow of seawater inhabited by strange little white and almost blind, crabs. These minute creatures are *munidopsis poliforma,* said to be unique in the underwater world. They are easily seen, looking like white stars glistening in the clear water or clinging to the rocks around the pool.

Across a narrow bridge beside the pool are more tables and chairs and another bar, even a discreet toilet tucked away amongst the rocks and plants. Up a flight of steps, daylight can be seen. An inviting swimming pool is available for anyone wanting a cool dip, but only glamorous bikini-clad young ladies seem to dare venture into the blue waters! All around the flora is of the most luxuriant variety and little rock pools are inhabited by turtles and ornamental fish, birds twitter and sing as they fly from one cavern to another.

Touring this singular attraction it is hard to believe that it is also a successful restaurant and night club. Twice a week the romantic cave is the scene of a stunning show of folk dancing and changing light patterns on the rocky lava walls and shining waters. It is said that Yehudi Menuhin has played his violin in the cave and found the acoustics perfect. The word *Jameos* means aperture and *Agua* is water, hence the name Jameos del Agua. Do not forget to take a coat and a camera. Men are required to wear a tie and jacket in the evening.

Continuing the journey southwards one leaves the area of lava rocks behind. On the coast **Arrieta** is fast getting a reputation with tourists as a place for excellent fresh fish meals. **Playa de la Garita** is still mostly deserted and a candidate for development.

One of the main features of Lanzarote is the black lava soil, which, with much ingenuity the islanders use to grow crops. Here vines are being cultivated in shallow holes of the picon soil, protected from the wind by low stone walls.

Reaching **Mala** and **Guatiza,** fields of prickly pears are seen, grown especially for the cochineal industry. It is in Lanzarote that the cochineal insect is cultivated. The species bred expressly for the dye is the *cocus cactu,* which lives on succulents like *nopal.* The farmer makes sure that the insects are suitably spread out amongst the plants where the female, almost unmoving on the plant, sucks up the juices of the cactus leaf. After three months the insects have reached full size and can be harvested. They are carefully scraped off the leaves and put in a box to kill them and shake off impurities. Afterwards they are dried in the sun prior to being packed in sacks for export. As a non-toxic substance, cochineal is used for colouring lipsticks, toothpaste and drinks like Campari. In the past this dye has been used for colouring woollen rugs.

Before finally reaching Arrecife again at the end of this tour a stop should be made at a massive new tourist development which is under construction five kilometres short of the capital, along the coast. This venture, called **Costa Teguise** is being made with the careful artistic direction of César Manrique. A complex of apartments and studios, in the light and airy Lanzarote style is set amongst lawns, gardens and swimming pools. Grouped in a typical village manner around a plaza are bungalows offering a more 'community' type of life style. The development includes supermarkets, bars and restaurants. Properties are available to rent or purchase. A further amenity is the 18-hole Costa Teguise Golf Course. Passes are issued to Lanzarote residents and to visitors for periods of one month, one week or a day.

One of the first buildings in the Costa Teguise development was the **Las Salinas Sheraton Hotel.** Designed to complement the local scenery, this five-star hotel is the epitome of luxury and comfort. The whole appearance is of a green oasis in a lava field. Outside are tall palm trees, tropical gardens, and a large swimming pool looking like a lake; balconies dripping with scarlet geraniums and bougainvillea blend with the white cantilevered building.

The cool marble hall is delightfully restful. Inside a large water garden is open to the skies and banks of tall grasses, ferns and shrubs, grow in profusion. Huge green plants trail from containers suspended from the three floors that surround the garden and pool; waterfalls, creating a feeling of opulence in such a dry island are enhanced at night by subtle coloured lighting.

Comfortable lounges, television room and bars are grouped spaciously. The dining room overlooks the sea and swimming pool. Three hundred and ten bedrooms and suites are furnished to a very high degree of comfort, with colour TV, radio and really private balconies. Included in the price of your room are around eighteen entirely free facilities, such as deep sea fishing, horseback riding, water ski, golf, archery, tennis, gymnasium and sauna. Evenings bring piano entertainments, cabaret, disco club and dancing.

Close to the hotel, **Playa de los Charcos** is a small sandy beach. If you are up early in the morning, you may be able to observe a family of Barbary partridge scurrying about for their early morning feed. Another bird to be seen in Lanzarote is the hoopoe, its bright pink, black and white striped plumage and noticeable erectile crest, make it easy to identify even without the characteristic deep 'hoo poo poo'.

From the Costa Teguise complex a fast coast road follows the coastline across arid wasteland, until it reaches Puerto de los Marmoles and Arrecife.

Lanzarote is in many ways an island that evades description. Impressive, widely contrasting, moon-like, sun drenched - all these phrases are true of its colourful volcanic landscape, full of vermillion, ochre, grey, black, blue and gold. But there is something beyond all this, some extraordinary and mysterious quality that fascinated everyone who comes here and that, after you have left, will make you yearn to return again to the Fire Island of Lanzarote.

9   Fuerteventura

Island of Solitude — Isla de Soledad

Fuerteventura is the second largest island in the Canary archipelago, and is, relatively, the least populated, with about 20,000 inhabitants to its area of 2020 sq km — half of whom live in Puerto del Rosario, the capital and main port.

North Africa is only about 90 km away and, indeed, Fuerteventura is very different from all the other islands because of its desert-like quality, looking and smelling much more like Morocco than Spain. A small mountain range runs down the middle north to south, its highest peak, **Pico de la Zarza** (807m) is in the southern peninsula of Jandia. This lack of high mountains accounts for the low rainfall and is the reason why winds in Fuerteventura can be strong at times, full of dust from Africa.

The great beauty of the island lies in its bare landscapes, with a shore line that includes vast white beaches — practically deserted — rocks, and extensive areas of sand dunes. The island is volcanic in origin, full of extinct volcanic cones, wide valleys and bare plains. Small villages with flat-topped houses are scattered widely, like green oases: just a few palm trees, a church, several bars and a small supermarket. Windmills draw a small amount of water from the subsoil and tomatoes, lettuce and some cereal crops are grown in the dry volcanic soil. Recently there has been an increase in the cultivation of tomatoes and at Gran Tarajal, in the south, a small boat runs a regular cargo of tomatoes to Las Palmas. The uncultivated land is grazed by goats. Although there are plenty of fish off the African coast the island has only a small fishing fleet, owing to its poor economic state.

However, it seems that tourism is going to be the answer to increasing prosperity. Since the building of its new airport, Los Estancos, south of Puerto del Rosario, Fuerteventura has been developing tourism. In the extreme north and south a few large hotels and apartments have been built and package tour holiday-makers are beginning to discover the delights of this unusual island. Fortunately it appears that, as in Lanzarote, the local authorities are maintaining tight control over development and keeping the building in style with the landscape.

It is now possible to tour the whole of Fuerteventura on reasonably good roads; only the more remote places still rely on sandy tracks across uneven scrubland. With little traffic on the roads, the main consideration has to be for the stray goats that always have priority of way in Fuerteventura — that is one of the characteristics that makes the island so appealing!

A regular inter-island passenger and car ferry sailing between Lanzarote and Las Palmas (Gran Canaria) puts into Puerto del Rosario three times a week. A small ferry operates between Corralejo, in the north, to Playa Blanca, Lanzarote.

Climate

Rainfall is very low and the island tends to be windy.

Temperatures never exceed 26°C in Summer and do not fall below 15°C in winter. The sea temperature remains constant at a comfortable 20°C all year. No Fuerteventura peasant is seen working in the fields without a straw hat with a large brim, reminding us that the sun's rays in Fuerteventura can be as much as 15 per cent stronger than on mainland Spain, so some protection is required initially, especially if one enjoys the pleasures of naturism, for which Fuerteventura beaches are so suitable.

Clothes — what to take

Lightweight clothes of the drip-dry variety are required. Some of the large hotels have laundry services, but do not expect launderettes if you are in an apartment. Beachwear is not allowed in dining rooms, although in the evenings dress is casual or trendy rather than formal. Take a windcheater jacket; your may decide to hire a jeep type car to tour the island, and winds can spring up quickly and become strong. There are very few clothes shops, but you will find boutiques where the big hotels are situated.

Accommodation

Accommodation in Fuerteventura is limited; even hotels on the tourist list may not be open all the year so it is advisable to write or telephone to check availability. In Puerto Rosario, the Hotel Valeron, Candelaria del Castillo, is two-star and has thirty rooms, sixteen of which are doubles with toilet and shower. With a seaview and in the centre of town, Hotel (residencia) Roque Mar, Plaza J. Dominguez Pena, has twenty rooms and a sitting room, but no catering facilities. Hotels and apartments in other resorts are mentioned in the tours sections.

The **Tourist Office** situated in the Avenida General Franco inside the building of Ministero de Trabajo (Ministry of Works) is on the first floor. Also in the Avenida General Franco the travel agent, Viajes Insular will make reservations for hotels, apartments, car hire, air and sea travel. The Aucona office for Trasmediterranea, the car and passenger ferry to Las Palmas and Lanzarote is located at the northern end of Calle Leon y Castillo. Open on Monday and Wednesday from 0900 to 1500 and 1700 to 1900 hrs. Tuesday and Thursday from 0900 to 1300. Saturday from 0900 to 1100 hrs.

Getting about the island

The public **bus service**, Transportes Fuerteventura, runs to all the main places on the island but the service is run mainly for farmers and their families, although it will stop for anyone at the roadside, if hailed. Do not be surprised if a goat goes along too! The bus from Puerto del Rosario to Corralejo in the extreme north leaves twice a day, a journey of thirty nine kilometres and costs 105 pesetas (54p) for the single fare. To go from the extreme south, Morro Jable to Puerto de la Cruz you would have to leave at 0600 hrs Puerto del Rosario, the journey takes two and a half hours, depending how often the driver stops for a chat. The bus returns south at 1400 hrs. So before you travel work out your route with plenty of time allowance. There is no service on a Sunday.

The main **taxi** rank is located on the seafront close to the port entrance and outside the Bar Tinguaro. In Fuerteventura all the taxis are coloured cream and green and carry four passengers. Fares are expensive, being 400 pesetas (£2) to the Aeropuerto los Estancos, a distance of five kilometres. From Puerto del Rosario to the Hotel Los Gorriones, Jandia, in the south, it is 3500 pesetas (£18) for a single journey. From Hotel los Gorriones to Gran Tarajal, 1600 pesetas (£8.24).

There are several **car-hire** firms in Puerto Rosario, including Autos Dominguez, Avenida General Franco 5, and Cita at Calle Almirante Lallemand 92. Open from 0800 to 1300 hrs and 1600 to 2000 hrs. Rates for a Seat 127 are about 1600 pesetas (£8.24) a day, plus 400 pesetas (£2) insurance and 2.7% tax. The price includes 100 kilometres free travel then a charge of 8 pesetas (4p) per kilometre.

Shopping

Most essential items are available in Puerto del Rosario, but it is wise to take as much as possible with you. Remember to stock up with English reading material; do not expect English newspapers in Fuerteventura.

Local hand-made embroidery can be purchased at Lajares in the north, also at El Molina in Antigua, the Artesania shop in Puerto del Rosario and at the bigger hotels. Other locally made souvenirs are basket-work, pottery and rag dolls. Homemade goats' cheese can be bought in Betancuria and in the market in Puerto del Rosario.

Generally prices of all goods are higher in Fuerteventura than in Gran Canaria and Tenerife, including all drinks. Should you wish to buy goats meat (*cabra*), most local butchers (*carniceria*) will have fresh supply. (*cabrito,* or roast kid, is delicious and like tender lamb). Fish is available, sometimes direct from the fishermens boats; however it is not especially cheap as demand from local people, restaurants, hotels and canning factories is high.

Banks in Puerto del Rosario are open from 0900 to 1300 hrs.

Restaurants and bars are of a simple nature, offering mostly Canarian food. For a more international cuisine it is necessary to visit the big hotels in the north and south.

History

The early inhabitants of Fuerteventura gave the island the name of Herbania, alluding to the thick vegetation found there, which has now almost completely disappeared. Nowadays it is species like euphorbia — cardon and tabaiba — and the cactus type plants which survive naturally.

As has already been stated the exact origin of the Guanches is still a subject for discussion. But in Fuerteventura some ethnic relationship with the Berbers of North Africa, and the people of the Iberian Peninsula can be observed. Like its neighbour Lanzarote, Fuerteventura had already been mapped when, in the early fifteenth century, the Frenchmen, Jean Bethencourt and Godifer de la Salle, set about conquering the island. For a period, the island belonged to the domain of the Lords of La Gomera, finally becoming Spanish National territory in 1496, with the conquest of Tenerife. Throughout the centuries Fuerteventura suffered terribly by raids from Algerian and Moorish pirates. At one time the Moors established their own communities on the island. Their influence can still be seen in the low square whitewashed houses and in some of the domes churches. These adversities helped to form the temperament of the people, patient and reserved, in a land of solitary and monotonous living, yet with a beauty of its own.

Today Fuerteventura belongs to the Province of Las Palmas, Gran Canaria, and slowly tourists are beginning to discover its immense beaches, and the serenity of its valleys, glinting red and brown in the constant sunshine. The inhabitants of its little village are tolerant and understanding of the tourist invasion for they realise the necessity of accepting this promise of prosperity to meet the needs of a modern Fuerteventura.

Puerto del Rosario, the capital and port

Puerto del Rosario, the capital of Fuerteventura, used to be called Puerto de las Cabras (Port of Goats), but in 1957 it was decided to improve its image by giving it a more attractive sounding name! Up to the end of the last century the island was divided into three municipalities, La Oliva, La Antigua and Betancuria, the last being the original capital of Fuerteventura.

The city is situated in a natural bay, with a small single-dock port. The atmosphere is that of a town that has settled by the sea. Seen from afar the skyline has little to commend it to the traveller, seeming to have become a little lost with its town planning. A new promenade is being constructed which will greatly improve the seafront area.

In the harbour fishing boats and small cargo ships jostle for space along the quay; the arrival of the Trasmediterranea ferry is a time of much activity. A few yachts make use of the calm waters of the bay. At the northern end of the town a large electricity power station stands on the edge of the coast. The garrison buildings, an important headquarters of the Spanish Foreign Legion, are a prominent feature of Puerto del Rosario. Impressive statues of foreign legionnaires are set in small gardens just off the Calle Almirante Lallemand.

Puerto Rosario, Capital of Fuerteventura. Quiet, clean, modern and friendly.

City tour

(Walking time about two hours)

The main street is Leon y Castillo which goes north from the seafront; the post office (*correos*) is halfway up on the left hand side. If you decide to have your mail sent to the post office, have it addressed with your surname first, then initials, followed by Lista de Correos, Puerto del Rosario, Fuerteventura. A special counter is headed *Lista de Correos*. Do not be surprised if you are handed the entire bundle of awaiting letters and asked to look for your own!

Close to the post office and at the crossroads of Calle General Franco and Gral Linares is the island's premier church, the Iglesia de la Virgen del Rosario. The principle fiesta on the island is to the Virgen del Rosario. held 1-7 October each year.

A market (*mercado*) is situated in the Plaza Espana, very small and clean with limited supplies of meat, fruit and vegetables. Fresh and tasty white goat's cheese can be bought whole or in a piece by weight. A turning off Calle General Franco called Calle Fuerteventura has a good butcher (*carniceria*) and next door a shop sells cooked chickens (*pollo asado*) and delicatessen foods.

Just up the road from the market is Artespana, the Spanish government handicraft shop, selling a small selection of costume dolls, children's toys, embroidered cloths, ceramics, pottery and basket-work, most of which is made in Fuerteventura. Prices compare favourably with the souvenir shops in the hotel resorts. In the *Artesania* shop you will probably find a young and pretty shop assistant who will be delighted to practise her English, is you speak slowly. English is now being taught in the schools to higher grade students, but because of the scarcity of English-speaking tourists, it is difficult for the language to be practised.

In Puerto del Rosario there is one discotheque, Taifa, in the Avenida Jose Antonio and one cinema, Marga, showing Spanish and Spanish-dubbed films.

Puerto del Rosario as the capital of Fuerteventura may seem to have little to offer the tourist but for the ardent traveller, it is a typical example of a quiet Canarian town. Going about their daily lives, the local people are always polite and helpful; often if there is a language problem — for very few speak English — they will go out of their way to show you your required destination, or find someone who is able to communicate with you.

For exploring the island, Puerto del Rosario makes a central base, with tourist areas and hotel accommodation being nearly equally divided between the extreme north and south.

Island tour 1 (north)

(Puerto del Rosario — Las Dunas — Corralejo — Isla de Los Lobos: about 29 km; full day including crossing to Los Lobos)

Taking the route northwards along the coast, the land is flat and sparse of vegetation. On the outskirts of Puerto del Rosario are the large electricity power station and the important desalination plant. Fish canning factories packing sardines and tuna fish, add considerably to the island economy. These are exported to the European market, and the quality of the fish canned makes it worth while seeking it out in the supermarkets.

A good road makes it a pleasant drive with seaviews the entire way to Corralejo, thirty eight kilometres north of Puerto del Rosario. Several small dirt-track roads lead down to little undeveloped bays and coves. The coast is earmarked for tourist development, however, and already several foreign entrepreneurs have started small urbanisations of villas. Many are unoccupied for much of the time and have a rather forlorn appearance. One of the new developments being built on the sea side of the road, near **Puerto Oliva,** is a sanatorium for people coming from Europe to recuperate in the sunshine and clear air of Fuerteventura.

Within fifteen kilometres of Corralejo, the landscape changes completely, for this is the area known as **Las Dunas** where sometimes the edges of the road can be obliterated by sand. Seen for the first time the great sand dunes on either side of the road can be quite stunning. This is the nearest thing to one's idea of a desert. It is a natural place of unique beauty, now designated as the **Parque Natural de las Dunas de Corralejo y la Isla de Los Lobos.** The site is an eco-system of great scientific value: the flora being resistant to strong winds and able to survive with little water and few nutrients. Regarding fauna, the main species is the lizard of Haria, endemic to Fuerteventura and Lanzarote, which though small has a large appetite and manages to eat quantities of the insects common to the Canary Islands. Bird life is plentiful close to the sea, in the sand dunes and this is a favourite resting place for migrating birds who seem to pass by night. Isla de Los Lobos is close by off the northern shore.

The beaches are entirely natural, with small rocky pools and clean water and are a marked contrast to the wild landscape of the interior. The light is brilliant for the sands are very fine, almost white, the sea a turquoise green, whilst above the blue sky rarely has a cloud. Just one warning: on rare occasions, when the *sirocco* blows and the skies are full of sand it is preferable to stay indoors with a good book!

188

Desertlike sands and warm blue seas are the background to the ultra modern hotel of Tres Islas, in the north of Fuerteventura. Excellent facilities and tranquil surroundings combine for a restful vacation.

Near the extreme north of the island just four kilometres before Corralejo, two magnificent hotels have been erected, looking rather out of place amongst the flatness of the area. Hotel Oliva Playa, three-star, and Hotel Tres Islas. four-star, both belong to the excellent hotel chain, Iberotel, which has vast experience of giving value for money in hotels in mainland Spain and the Balearic Islands as well as the Canary Islands. Three islands — Fuerteventura, Los Lobos and Lanzarote — can indeed be seen from the Hotel Tres Islas which is set right on the sand dunes at the edge of the blue Atlantic, with all that is expected of a first class hotel. At present visitors are mostly from Germany and Scandinavia, so most of the entertainments and menus are geared for their pleasure. Nevertheless, when you make it known that you are British, an attentive staff including English-speaking members will endeavour to make you feel welcome. There is plenty of sport and entertainment during the day for young and more mature holidaymakers, offering alternatives to the beach or hotel pools: video shows and dancing nightly in the hotel or disco, quiz games, folk dancing and cabaret shows provide some of the attractions. Prices in the hotel bar are reasonable; a small beer or mineral costs 75 pesetas (38p). Cointreau liqueur 130 pesetas (67p), whisky 225 pesetas (£1.16) and champagne cocktail 200 pesetas (£1).

Round-the-island coach tours lasting all day and including lunch cost 1700 pesetas (£8.76) and are very good value, enabling tourists to see inside churches that are usually closed during the day except on Sunday. Other excursions are a visit to Los Lobos island, 1600 pesetas (£8.24); a 'Safari Jeep' drive which goes along unmade roads to little known beaches, 2700 pesetas (£14). Another popular outing is to visit the island of Lanzarote, going by Alisur Ferry from Corralejo to Playa Blanca in the south of Lanzarote and continuing round the island by coach, visiting the major interest. The price from Corralejo is 3900 pesetas (£20), from Jandia in the south, 5100 pesetas (£26). To include lunch, add another 1000 pesetas (£5).

Close to the hotels are some apartments, two supermarkets and a boutique. Both apartment blocks have travel agents, Viajes Insular and Viajes Ultramar Express, where the staff have a reasonable knowledge of English and are helpful.

Driving around the north eastern tip of Fuerteventura, the bright white sand dunes continue while the Atlantic rollers increase as they surge through the channel called El Rio, which divides Fuerteventura and **Isla de Los Lobos.**

This is a place much favoured by naturists who use discreet areas in the sand dunes for total sun bathing. Wind surfing is much in evidence in all the Canary Islands, especially so in Fuerteventura off the *playas* of Corralejo (and down south off the Jandia peninsula). Several good fish restaurants are to be found along the beaches where you can sit on the patio looking out over the translucent waters towards Lobos and the volcanic peaks of Lanzarote, while your fresh fish is being barbecued. Restaurant la Galera has an international menu and is open late in the evening. Close by the Corintia Restaurant is owned by Don Demetrio who will ensure that you have an enjoyable meal.

The area around Corralejo is being developed into a major tourist resort, with projected hotels and apartments going up in all directions. Sailing, underwater swimming and windsurfing provide plenty of outdoor sport. Along the shores the sandy beaches and rocky inlets are of much interest to crab hunters and shell collectors.

Corralejo, once a small lively fishing village, has gained in importance with the extension of the harbour; now it is used not only by fishing boats which go as far as the Sahara coast, but by the ferry to Lanzarote and excursion boats to Lobos. An increasing number of yachts and pleasure boats are using its facilities.

The small town has several supermakets, tourist shops and all the usual utilities, including travel agents, taxi and car hire, petrol station, garage and banks. As well as apartment complexes, where they have their own supermarkets, there is a one-star Hotel Corralejo, 35 bedrooms, overlooking the sea and providing simple and clean accommodation. There is a selection of restaurants and bars, Freddies Disco being very popular at night.

Coach tours that stop in Corralejo always recommend tourists to enjoy the splendid ice cream dishes and cheesecakes that are especially prepared for holidaymakers.

Isla de Los Lobos takes its name from the seals (lobos marinos) which once haunted the local waters. It is said that Godifer de la Salle, a Norman knight, was marooned here during an expedition to Lanzarote and that he survived only by killing and eating seals.

From Corralejo the tiny island is only three kilometres off shore, it lies in the waters known as the Bocaina, derived from the Spanish word *boca* (mouth) because the waters are so full of fish that they surge along like a 'mouthful'. The fishing in the area is said to be the best in the Canaries and can be done from a boat or with snorkel and harpoon.

The island, which is 6.5 sq kms, is used by fishermen who have formed a community at El Puertito on the east coast. Excursions from Corralejo take tourists to the island for swimming and a beach barbecue.

Island tour 2 (north)

(Corralejo — Lajares — Cotillo — La Oliva — Tetir — Puerto de Rosario: about 73 km; half day drive)

Nine kilometres south of Corralejo, on the GC600, a turning west goes to Lajares and Cotillo. This is a rather narrow road which goes through lava rock and *malpais* (wastelands) created by volcanic eruptions; yet one can see where in the past much effort has been made to try and cultivate the soil. Small fields are marked out with lava stone walls, even the odd fig tree is encircled to stop the goats from browsing its green leaves. Ruins of old stone houses, evidence of past habtitation, look sad and lost. Every now and then a herd of goats will meander along the road, oblivious of travellers and one wonders what they will find to chew because, apart from the *Ulaga* (thorn bush) there is little else to be seen. However all the goats seem to be in very good condition and grow to a huge size, looking very fiercesome with curved horns and long shaggy beards, and coats which are a thick mixture of brown, black and white hair.

Lajares is a small cluster of farmers' houses, with a bar and supermarket. A new tourist attraction has been opened recently as it is a convenient stopping place for coach parties: a small School of Embroidery allows visitors to watch the nimble-fingered ladies sewing the intricate open drawn thread work that is typical of the Canaries. With deft hands they sit at a long wooden frame, the cloth drawn tightly across, as their fingers flick in and out with amazing speed — nevertheless a time-consuming task in these days of machinery. The tablecloths are expensive to buy but are a real joy to possess and with care can last a life-time. A small tourist shop next door offers an assortment of locally made articles.

The windmill just north of La Oliva, used both for grinding corn and pumping water.

From Lajares it is seven kilometres to **Cotillo,** a small fishing village on the north west coast of Fuerteventura. The village has some narrow one-way streets. A seventeenth century watchtower La Torre de Rico Roque is a Feature. To the north of the village is a series of quiet sandy beaches and fishing can be had from the rocky points. This area has been earmarked for tourist developments, its lonely peaceful location having great appeal for those who appreciate solitude and remoteness.

Returning by the same road to Lajares, it is possible to take a turning to La Oliva ten kilometres south. As one leaves Lajares behind, the road affords a splendid view of windmills depicting two different uses — the one on the left is for corn grinding, while the other is for pumping water from the subsoil.

La Oliva is a noble town which has played an important part in the history of the island. Many aborigine artefacts have been found within the municipality, including fertility idols which the ancient races worshipped. In the fifteenth century the Norman conquistadors, Jean de Bethencourt and Godifer de la Salle used La Oliva as a base for further conquests. When, in 1703, the Canary Islands ceased to be ruled by the nobility and passed to a central government in Tenerife, the ruling military officer, the 'Colonel' who was in charge in La Oliva, became a person of great importance, in fact the chief personage on the island.

The Casa de los Coroneles (Mansion of the Colonels) was for many years the centre of social and political life in Fuerteventura. This magnificent structure remains to testify to the importance of La Oliva in the past. When in the nineteenth century the port of Cabras (now Puerto del Rosario) grew in importance, the political and economic life of the island moved there.

The Casa de Los Coroneles, which belongs to the Bravo de Laguna family, is now being restored. This old fortress palace has a facade that includes a coat of arms, crowned by a small cross. Carved wooden balconies line the front of the building, two turrets at each end give a picture of symmetrical balance. It is reputed that the original building contained 365 doors and windows; we shall have to see if they are still there when the restoration is completed!

The Casa del Capellan (Chaplain's House), a smaller palace, is also of note. It has a huge wooden door decorated with Aztec designs thought to have been influenced by seafaring merchants visiting Mexico and Latin America.

The only religious building in La Oliva is the parish church, Iglesia de Nuestra Señora de Candelaria. A sturdy fortress-like stone building, white washed, except for the tall bell tower, it stands in a prominent position, its buttressed exterior walls, giving evidence of its past use as a sanctuary from marauding pirates. Inside, its enormous proportions contain three naves, which have paintings by Juan de Miranda. There are many carvings of the saints. The holy relic of the image of Nuestra Señora de Candelaria is kept high above the altar.

On the second of February each year, in La Oliva, a fiesta is held to honour the Virgen de la Candelaria (of Tenerife). This is a four-day celebration of religious fervour and joyful festivity. The first day the religious relic is paraded, held on a dais at shoulder level, by four men. With due solemnity it is taken round the church square, while prayers are said and hymns are sung.

In the afternoon and during the next two days there are many sports events, children's and folk dancing. It culminates on the last day with the events like Canary Wrestling, and a fireworks display. The entire town enters into this festive occasion, all dressed in new clothes. Wine flows freely, bands play and it is a gay, animated scene set under cloudless skies. Everyone, including tourists, is welcome to join in the celebrations and the Carnival.

In La Oliva there are a few bars but no restaurants; the nearest is in Playa de Corralejo. A post office and small shop is situated at the northern end of the main street.

Around the town is a wide plain and various sisal plantations are seen, this being one of the main agricultural products of Fuerteventura. Old windmills and grazing goats make up the sparse scenery. Towards the mountains rabbits, partridge, turtle doves, pigeons and exotic Gangas, a species of African game bird exclusive to the island, give a little sport for the hunters.

Continuing the journey south from La Oliva on the GC600, a turning off westwards leads to **Tindaya,** a small town of pleasant simplicity in an extremely dry area. **Montana Quemada** (the burnt mountain) rises out of the flat plain, notable as the place where a monument has been erected to honour Miguel de Unamuno (1864-1936), the great Spanish thinker and writer, who was exiled to Fuerteventura because of his political views. His love of the island, its peace and beauty, led to many eloquent verses. 'A rock thirsting in the sun Fuerteventura, a treasure of health and honesty, may God guard you for ever from super abundance'.

A secondary road leads off from the GC600 just south of the Unamuno monument which is a short route to Betancuria, the old capital, but on that road you will drive through really wild desert scenery. The Prison Agricultural Colony near Tefia is making an effort to cultivate the plain but it is a difficult project.

The GC600 continues southwards to **Tetir,** formerly a separate municipality but today part of the island's capital. The town is in a wide valley where some of the main cereal crops are grown. In the distance, looking north, the mountain called the Devil's Claw can be seen, a title explained by the dark spiky shapes. From Tetir it is but nine kilometres to the capital Puerto del Rosario.

Island tour 3 (central)

(Puerto del Rosario — Casillas del Angel — La Ampungenta — La Antigua — Tuineje — Pajara — Betancuria — Valle Santa Inés — Llanos de la Concepción — Puerto del Rosario: about 83 km; full day's drive)

A central tour of the island can be made from Puerto del Rosario, taking an inland highway, the GC160, westwards from the city in the direction of La Antigua. The first place of importance is **Casillas del Angel** with its unusual neo-colonial style church. It has a bell tower of black masonry. The little village is scattered around in a rather haphazard manner.

A short distance further on is **La Ampungenta,** with its walled church of San Pedro de Alcantara. There the road divides with a detour going to Betancuria, the main road continuing south to La Antigua. On the outskirts of this town is **El Molino** (the windmill), now a premier stopping point for all tourist excursions. This two-hundred-year-old windmill is now fully restored and makes a beautiful picture. Visitors are allowed inside to see the corn being ground, and a custodian will do his best to explain the workings. There is a large car park.

Set in attractive gardens full of cactus, flowers and shrubs, is a large restaurant and bar. A small gift shop sells a range of simple hand-made souvenirs; the lady in the shop is busy with her hand-drawn needlework when not serving customers. Meals are served quickly in the restaurant and prices are average. The toilets are clean. If you only want a snack, try the soup: it is almost a meal and very tasty. For a cool drink ask for *Sangria,* which is always served in a jug for two or more. Consisting usually of red wine, brandy, sparkling mineral water, lots of cut up oranges and lemons, with ice cubes it is a typical Spanish drink. About 300 pesetas (£1.50).

La Antigua is a large village with a definite African flavour: low white-washed houses have flat roofs and shuttered windows. Many of the side roads are unmade tracks; dogs, chickens and goats wander about but few people are seen. Tall palm trees and small plantations of alfalfa (used for animal feeding) make patches of brilliant green; a few vegetables are cultivated, water being drawn from the wells.

In some outlying areas, with the improvement of water drainage systems and the use of desalinated water (taken from the sea), tomatoes are now being grown as individual undertakings by families adding to their meagre income.

Going further south along the GC160, one has fine views of the low reddish-brown mountains, the bright light casting shadows in patterns of different hues. The open vistas and space on every side creates a feeling of peace and relaxation. This is not a drive for anyone craving excitement, unless you enjoy dodging goats! Should you be in need of refreshment, make a stop at a small wayside bar restaurant which lies by itself at the side of the main road, a few kilometres north of **Agua de Bueyes.** Bar Gaira is typical of many Canarian bars: from the outside unobtrusive and quiet and inside all modern, gleaming and clean. Whether you have drinks and tappas (snacks) at the bar or order a meal at the table, the service will be polite and friendly. Should you wonder what to order, the *senor* will be delighted for you to step into the kitchen, where his wife and daughter will smile happily as your nose advises you which of the tasty stews to select. You could be surprised at the reasonable bill at the end of the meal.

A few miles on is **Tuineje,** site of the historic battle of Tamasite against the English pirates. (All seems forgiven these days!)

Our central tour goes no further south but turns westwards to Pajara on the GC620, passing several ruined dwellings, for it is a place of past agricultural activity. When the road reaches **Toto,** situated in a narrow valley, the sudden sight of waving palm trees and small areas of cultivation is welcome after the harshness of the arid fields and lava stone walls. In the warm shelter of the valley, tomatoes and vegetables are grown, bright bougainvillea and poinsettia bloom outside the little square white washed houses.

Betancuria, the old capital of the island, so remote, attracts many tourists who always visit the old cathedral, Iglesia de Santa Maria, rebuilt in the early seventeenth century on a grand scale. It still has an air of its past magnificence.

The Aztec designs on the carved stone portal are an interesting
feature of the church at Pajara, presumably the work of a sixteenth
century craftsman who had returned from the New World.

Pajara (meaning little bird) is noted especially for its parish church. The main entrance (just off the main road) has Aztec style sculptures over its huge doors. The shapes of suns, serpents, pumas and plumed crowned heads are carved in stone. The mixture of Gothic and Aztec designs dating from the mid sixteenth century are a fascinating sight in such a remote place. The stone work is in good order and the blocks have a perfect fit. The main entrance is topped by a triangular pediment. Inside the church the high altar dates from the eighteenth century. There is also an interesting Baroque confessional box, its dark wood heavily carved. There is no parking problem in the village.

Leaving Pajara one starts to view some of the finest mountain scenery in the island. The route is along a rather narrow road with a reasonably good surface and steep bends penetrating high into the mountain range. All round the rich red soil is bare, but for cactus struggling to grow in the rock crevices. As greater heights are reached there are immense panoramas of old, extinct volcanic peaks, some in curious shapes, all bathed in a warm glow of sunlight.

The purity of the air and the stillness are part of the magic that is Fuerteventura. At certain point on the road the coastline is seen, with the Atlantic stretching out endlessly, presenting a contrasting colour. The highest point has a view of the **Canyon del Rio Palma** and the **Canyon de la Pena.** In the valley is a sanctuary of the Virgin of Sorrows, patron saint of Fuerteventura. The fifteenth century alabaster image of Our Lady is much revered; a pilgrimage is made every September and people travel from all over the island to worship at the shrine.

After reaching a height of about some six hundred metres the road starts to descend and some vegetation is seen with the occasional homestead. Here and there a lonely fig tree, with its stone wall encirclement, flourishes — even the odd almond tree will be in blossom if you travel that way in January.

The ancient capital of Feurteventura, Santa Maria de **Betancuria**, lies 27 kms south west of Puerto del Rosario, and is still the second place of importance in the island. It was founded by the Norman conqueror, Jean de Bethencourt in 1402; he felt that is was safer to live in the centre of the island away from attacking pirates. Hidden away in the heart of the mountains, this historic old town has now been declared a national monument. All that remains of its past glory is a quiet little community of about five hundred inhabitants and a large number of goats, but with some historical monuments which are well worth seeing.

Arriving at Berancuria by the road from Pajara, the Museo Arqueologico is on the right side of the main road. This is a real delight to visit, even those who do not usually like museums will enjoy walking round this tiny treasury of ancient historic relics. The first room is not unusual with its skulls and bones of bygone Guanches, and bowls, tools and weapons to give an idea of their way of life. In a further room a picture of Jean de Bethancourt helps to fill the history of events, swords and goblets showing the grandeur of the nobility. But it is outside in the stone paved courtyard that the spell of the past is felt, in the tiny stone-floored rooms where ancient cooking utensils, agricultural tools and furniture are all displayed in a delightfully casual array.

Upstairs (mind the rickety staircase) there is a tiny room with a four-poster bed, looking just as it must have looked when last used. A wee pot and a small pair of lady's dainty high-heeled shoes are under the bed. It is quite the most informal museum you will ever enjoy. Outside stand two bronze cannon.

A little further down the road on the same side as the museum is the Mayor's house. Opposite, there is a small bar with a cool patio and tables set for meals. It has a car park and toilet.

Continuing along the main street which winds over a dry river bed, the mighty edifice of the cathedral, Iglesia de Santa Maria de Betancuria stands high above. In the fifteenth century Bethencourt built a church which was the first episcopal seat in the archipelago, but it was destroyed by fire in 1539 by Berber Corsairs and the cathedral we see today was built in the seventeenth century. Its architectural style shows a strong Moorish influence with small windows and graceful tower. But gracing the sidewall is a very fine example of a typical Canarian pine wood balcony, beautifully carved. In the cathedral patio the deep well still has water.

The cathedral building is perfectly white washed. It has an imposing and highly decorated carved wooden doorway. Inside, the high altar is seventeenth century Baroque and three vaulted niches catch the eye, two saints at the side with the Virgin and Child in the centre. At the rear of the cathedral deeply ornamented chairs are set like thrones under a wooden canopy, these were used by the nobility in days gone by. To one side is the image of Saint Buenaventura set on a plaque, this is much venerated and is paraded at the Fiesta on 14th July each year.

Much of Fuerteventura is dry, hot and dusty, but the occasional
vegetation of palm and cactus create a landscape of peaceful charm.

It is said that, because of past sieges, there are hideaway holes and escape doors set high in the roof. Underneath the huge flagstone floor are the tombs of past Betancurians. In the sacristy are kept many precious relics: the Conquest Banner, Archbishop's regalia, crosses and candlesticks. A further chapel is now under restoration, its walls have wonderful murals, depicting religious scenes.

A few yards from the cathedral is a souvenir shop, and the lady there is the custodian of the cathedral and has the keys. When coach parties arrive she gives a demonstration of how goats' cheese is made; this may be purchased in the shop.

Walk along the valley road a little further and you will see the ruins of a Franciscan Monastery in which lived the Saint Diego de Alcala, who preached the gospel in the Canary Islands, especially to the sick and the poor, and was canonized in 1558. Now only a single Gothic window, a few columns and some outer walls remain. On the other side of the valley is the recently restored Ermita de San Diego de Alcala, a hermitage built over a cave where the Spanish monk prayed. Further restoration is being done by the Ministry of Culture to a former convent which lies on the hill at the back of the village. This will eventually house an important library and archives.

Driving northwards from Betancuria the road again gives very fine panoramic views over the mountain ranges. There is a feeling of being on top of the world as the road affords vistas across to the sea on both sides of the island at once, with the bare red rocks of the mountains and valley in between.

Passing through **Valle Santa Inés,** with its cluster of palm trees and **Llanos de la Concepción,** the road descends to the flat plains below and continues on to Casillas del Angel, which we visited on the outward trip, and back to Puerto del Rosario.

Island tour 4 (south)

(Puerto del Rosario — Aeropuerto Estanca — Caleta de Fuste — Pozo Negro — La Antigua — Las Playitas — Gran Tarajal: about 97 km; half day's drive)

An alternative to taking the GC610 to the south of the island, is to leave Puerto del Rosario on the coastal highway marked *Aeropuerto.* It is only a short distance to Playa Blanca with its small sandy beach. Close by is the Parador Nacional, at present being enlarged and modernised. Set by the sea it has good views towards Puerto del Rosario. The small Aeropuerto Estanca is located at sea level. Charter aircraft arrive daily throughout the year from Europe. There is a daily service to Las Palmas, Tenerife and Lanzarote and a weekly flight direct to Seville and Madrid by Iberia Airways.

Continuing on the road southwards, **Caleta de Fuste** is one of the most important tourist areas, with two developments that are in use. The entrance to one block has flags of six nations, but the Union Jack has yet to be added!

The old *Castillo* is an eighteenth century watch tower around which an urbanisation has grown. With swimming pool and tennis courts, restaurants and shops the area seems self-contained. Two tier accommodation consists of a lounge, kitchen with eating bar, twin-bedded room and good bathroom facilities. It is well equipped with crockery, cutlery, fridge but no cooker. Rent is 1450 pesetas (£7.50) per person per day; gas, water and electricity is included.

Caleta de Fuste's small harbour has a good yacht marina with water and electric points and two hard slipways with launching bay. The gates are locked at night. The sandy beach is in between the two developments and wind surfing is available with equipment for hire and tuition for beginners. It should be mentioned that Fuerteventura can suffer strong winds.

The coast road then turns inland and goes across old *Malpais* (volcanic wasteland) but, being a new road, the surface is good. As there is very little traffic, travel can be fast. Occasionally one sees a small dwelling where, apart from a couple of chickens and a dog, the only sign of life is the inevitable herd of goats. At a signposted junction a turning goes east to **Pozo Negro,** eleven kilometres away, at present devoid of any modern development. It is not possible to continue south on a tarmac road from Pozo Negro. The other branch at the junction goes north and heads for La Antigua where one can join the C610 southwards through Tuineje to Gran Tarajal.

The newly built yacht marina at Caleta de Fuste, a developing tourist resort on the east coast of Fuerteventura.

A typical warm, but sometimes windy, deserted Fuerteventura beach, ideal sunbathing.

Two kilometres before Gran Tarajal, at the beginning of a palm grove, a turning to the left takes you eastwards to **Las Playitas.** This is a delightful small fishing village in a sheltered bay. At the southern end a deserted greyish sandy beach is reached by going down a dirt track road; there swimming is possible when the sea is calm.

The main part of the village is clustered at the eastern end of the bay, which lies under a high cliff face. With only a shallow pebble and rock beach, it is used mainly by the local fishermen who go out daily in their fragile one-man boats, some of which have engines. It is a tightly knit Canarian community whose main income is from the sea. The upright young men are tall and proudly good looking, and they work long hard hours. When a boat returns from fishing the whole family and friends rush out to help drag it ahsore. Excitedly the children are allowed to look at the catch first. Later they are expected to assist with cleaning out the boat. The fish is put on the beach to be weighed, gutted and sold. Restaurants, hotels, fish-canning factories and family come first, but should there be any left, the tourist may be able to purchase the fish. On occasions the catch is sufficiently large for quantities of fish, usually sardines, to be prepared for drying. It is a labourious task to gut and split open the tiny fish, which are then laid out on wire racks to dry in the sunshine and sprinkled with salt. Later on they are stored in boxes. The Canarians will eat these dried fish raw and consider them a tasty *tappa* (snack).

A small contingent of Scandinavians have bought holiday homes around Las Playitas; they appear to mingle pleasantly with the local community. A bar in the village is very clean and simple meals are available.

The name of **Gran Tarajal,** is taken from the tamarisk trees that grow in the area. The town is a busy commercial centre with many shops, supermarkets, garage, cinema, post office and banks. Cafes and bars are found along the seafront, but surprisingly there are no hotels. Its good harbour makes it of great importance to the south of the island; it is second only to Puerto del Rosario for the export of tomatoes, which are grown and packed locally. A large beach has fine blackish sands and a pleasant paved promenade.

Weighing fish on primitive scales is an important moment for the fishermen of Fuerteventura.

The fishing village of Playitis. A few apartments are available here.
It is a few miles N.E. of Gran Tarajal.

Island tour 5 (south)

Gran Tarajal — Tarajalejo — Playa de la Pared — Costa Calma — Playa Jandia — Morro Jable: about 69 km; half day's drive)

Two kilometres north of Gran Tarajal, a well surfaced road runs westwards to the next place of any note, **Tarajalejo Playa.** The village is a small Canarian community. A forlorn seafront from which three or four local fishing boats go out each day, is very neglected. In the village three bars have restaurant space where good fish meals are served. All is simple, with plastic tablecloths, and the atmosphere is mostly Canarian. Price of an average fish dish is 400 pesetas (£2). A single supermarket is the only shop in Tarajalejo.

On the edge of the village, going southwest, a golden sandy beach is suitable for swimming. A German-owned three-star hotel, the Maxorata, is set back a few metres off the main coast road. Pleasantly appointed and small it is used mostly by Germans, its main attraction being its close proximity to the sandy beach. A double room costs 2000 pesetas (£10) per night, inclusive meals are an extra 1000 pesetas (£5) per person per day. The hotel, being so isolated, is suitable for peaceful holidays. The hire of a car would be necessary for exploring the island, unless taxis are used (rather expensive).

A few yards from this hotel are some apartments, available for renting, Apartamentos Matorral. Of modern design they consist of a bedroom, kitchen, lounge, bathroom and balcony or patio. Cost per night for a one-bedroom apartment is 2000 pesetas (£10) including water and electricity.

Just before the road reaches the little fishing village of La Lajita, there is a splendid panoramic view of the southern part of Fuerteventura. In the distance is the light brown rocky mountain range known as Las Orejas de Asno (The Asses' Ears) of which Pico de Zarza at 807 m is the highest peak. But it is the vast stretch of sand dunes and its golden sandy beaches, with their shallow turquoise waters, which makes a lasting impression: a great open space so beautiful and full of peace.

The scenery becomes progressively more desert like as one reaches **Matas Blanca,** nine and a half kilometres south of Tarajalejo. This is the area known as the **Jandia Peninsula.** Many centuries ago a dividing wall marked two separate Guanche kingdoms, Maxorata and Jandia. Today a metal road shows the route across the sand dunes and scrubland, and the glare of the sun on the vast sands reminds us of the closeness of Africa.

210

The native breed of dog, called Bardinos, bears little resemblance to its ferocious ancestors. They are gentle in behaviour but make good watch dogs when trained. This cheerful fellow gives a friendly welcome to tourists who visit Betancuria.

A small signpost by the main road marks the road to Playa de la Pared on the west coast; at this point the peninsula is only five kilometres wide.

Across the west coast (windwardside) at **Playa de la Pared** is the Atlantida Club, a small German owned apartment hostel; price is 2000 pesetas (£10) for a twin-bedded apartment. The Club is in a most isolated position; the coastline is very rocky, and swimming can be dangerous because of strong currents. However good fishing is possible from the rocks, when the sea is not too fierce. Nearby **Playa de Barlovento de Jandia** is without metal roads, except from La Pared. Steep crumbling sandstone cliffs make access to the beaches very difficult. It is advisable to retrace one's route to the main road.

At **Costa Calma** (a road sign denotes the area) the developers are beginning to build tourist complexes. As yet, most of it is in the planning stage with notices saying *Se Vende* (for sale) on plots of land. At one such venture, called Solyventura apartments are being constructed close to the immense flat beach. In time this is expected to be a self-contained community with shops, swimming pool, sports centre and entertainments.

A few yards from the Costa Calma signpost, a bar restaurant Taverna Costa Calma lies at the roadside. This little establishment is one recommended by the hotel couriers. Take advantage of what it has to offer, as eating places are few and far between in Fuerteventura. Clean red check tablecloths and prompt service help to make this a pleasant venue. A *paella* for two will cost 1,200 pesetas (£6), fish 400 pesetas (£2), a steak 475 pesetas (£2.44), half a litre of beer or a mineral, 75 pesetas (38p).

Playa de Sotovento de Jandia, on the leewardside, has the twenty-two kilometre stretch of unbroken sands for which Fuerteventura is so famed. These vast fine grained sands are mostly deserted except for sea birds that fly over from Africa to feed in the lagoons that are formed at low tide; egrets, sandpipers and curlews can be seen, and in the sand dunes the hoopoe birds make a startling splash of colour.

At **Playa de la Barca** (79 kilometres from Puerto del Rosario and 15 kilometres south of Gran Tarajal) the three-star hotel Los Gorriones is well signposted and has been built right on the beach, standing out like a white castle. This luxury hotel belongs to the Hotasa group of Spanish hoteliers and is used by package holiday tour operators. It has 326 bedrooms with private bathrooms and balconies (most with sea views), and all the facilities of a modern, self-contained, hotel, including shops, sports facilities and nightly entertainment. As well as the hotel restaurant there is a separate *a la carte* restaurant open in the evenings, serving international cuisine. Try the Chateaubriand, 1600 pesetas (£8.24), for two persons.

Excursions by coach from the hotel include: around the island sightseeing, 1500 pesetas (£7.70); sand dune party, 1300 pesetas (£6.70) including food, wine and music; a Jeep Safari which visits small beaches, 1500 pesetas (£7.70); a shark fishing trip from Morro Jable, 2000 pesetas (£10). Cars may be hired from the hotel: a Seat 127 for the day costs 1750 pesetas (£9) plus insurance and cost of petrol. A hotel bus runs once a week into Gran Tarajal for tourists to shop. A taxi from the hotel to Puerto del Rosario costs 3500 pesetas (£18) for a single journey. This is very much a hotel for anyone who requires a quiet and peaceful ambience with comfortable accommodation. The beach is tranquil — ideal for naturist swimming and sunbathing.

El Esquinzo, Stella Maris and **Playa Jandia,** further south, all have small complexes of apartments and villas, with further developments in various stages of building progress along the coast. Very little traffic makes for pleasant driving, but if it is windy watch out for sand that can obliterate the edges of the road.

At **Playa Jandia** two hotels, the four-star Casa Atlantica and the three-star Robinson Club, are used mainly by German tourists; both are situated close to the beach. A nearby modern shopping complex has a boutique, hairdressing salon, supermarket, souvenir shops and travel agents. Two small bars serve meals: everywhere notices are written in Spanish and German and it is hard to find anyone who will speak English. No cars are allowed to park on the beach or in the sand dunes. A wind surfing school, which operates from the beach at Playa Jandia, is very popular.

Three kilometres along the main road is the fishing village of **Morro Jable;** a larger than average community with improved facilities since the advent of tourists. There is a bank, several large supermarkets, post office, petrol station and garage, it has much importance. (For similar services it is a 52 kilometre drive to Gran Tarajal.) However there is need for more parking space, and it may be necessary to leave your transport on the outskirts and walk to the shops and beach.

Morro Jable has a high reputation with tourists for its fish meals. Two cafés have terraces where food may be eaten in the sunshine. A very narrow road leads to the beach, where local fishermen keep their small boats with the nets spread out over the sands. Often the fish is put out to dry, making it a very pictorial scene. It is possible to walk from Morro Jable to Hotel Los Gorriones, a distance of twenty-one kilometres along the wide sandy beach — a super walk but you will need a rest and a drink afterwards! At present the tarmac road continues past Morro Jable for just 2 kilometres along the coast and then a dirt track for 15 kilometres leads to the lighthouse at Punta de Jandia, the extreme south west of Fuerteventura; here cliffs and a rocky beach mark the end of the land.

Fuerteventura is not a place for those who like bright lights and noisy entertainments on their holiday. There is little to do but swim and sunbathe, unless you are energetic and like to windsurf, fish or enjoy underwater swimming. It is very much a place where one 'gets away from it all', a wonderful land, full of light and mellow colours, of open vistas, where the local people accept the needs of the tourist without resentment, yet continue to retain their own traditions and crafts.

Off the beaten track, Fuerteventura is one of the places where true wilderness remains yet can be visited by the traveller, an island of solitude.

Finale

The Canary Islands are easy to enjoy. Natural beauties abound, and the longer you stay the more you will have the opportunity to discover and delight in the vast variety. Whatever your age and interests it is probably that you will be able to indulge in your favourite pastime here. The majority of people visit the Canaries for warmth and sunshine. The fact that the tourist industry is ever increasing is a sure sign that visitors are not disappointed.

Mountain peaks, green valleys, busy cities, dusty deserts, restful beaches, palm trees and exotic flowers, entertainments, solitude, service and smiles, all are here in the enchanting Canary Islands. These 'Fortunate Islands' are truly a continent in miniature where the splendours of nature are combined with the modern conveniences that we have all come to accept as part of our lives.

For us, the Canary Islands will always be thought of as the Friendly Islands. We hope that this will be your happy experience too.

Appendix A — Spanish English Vocabulary

Public Signs and Notices

abierto	— open
aseo	— toilet
caballeros	— gentlemen
cerrado	— closed
empuje	— push
entrada	— entrance
libre	— free/vacant
muelle	— quay
ocupado	— engaged
privado	— private
salida	— depart/way out
senoras	— ladies
se alquilar	— to rent
se prohibe	— forbidden
servicio	— toilet
se vende	— for sale
se prohibe estacioner	no parking
se prohibe fumar	— no smoking
tire	— pull

Drinks

Beer	Cerveza
Coffe/Black	Café Solo
Coffee/white	Café con Leche
Gin	Ginebra
Ice	Hielo
Sherry	Jerez
Squash	Zumo
Tea	Té
Water	Agua
Wine dry	Vino seco
red	Vino tinto
sweet	Vino dulce
white	Vino blanco

Shops and places

Baker	Panaderia
Butcher	Carniceria
Cake shop	Pasteleria
Chemist	Farmacia
Church	Iglesia
Cinema	Cine
Dairy	Lecheria
Fishmonger	Pescaderia
Grocer	Alimentacion
Ironmonger	Ferreteria
Library	Biblioteca
Market	Mercado
Post Office	Correos
Shoe shop	Zapateria
Stationer	Papelaria
Theatre	Teatro
Town Hall	Ayuntamiento
View Point	Mirador

Restaurant

Bill	Cuenta
Bottle	Botella
Breakfast	Desayuno
Cup	Taza
Dinner	Cena
Drink	Bebida
Fork	Tenedor
Glass	Vaso
Knife	Cuchillo
Lunch	Almuerzo
Plate	Plato
Sandwich	Bocadillo
Spoon	Cuchara
Table	Mesa
Tip	Propina
Waiter	Camarera

Useful Words

All	Todo
Before	Antes
Behind	Detras
Big	Grande
Cold	Frio
Everybody	Todos
Fast	Rapido
Food	Alimento
Good	Bueno
Here	Aqui
High	Alto
Hot	Caliente
How many?	Cuantos
How much?	Cuanto
Left (direction)	Izquierda
Like	Como
Little (quantity)	Poco
Lost	Perdido
Many	Mas
Near	Cerca
No	No
Old	Viejo
Please	Por favor
Right (direction)	Derecha
Slow	Lento
Soon	Pronto
Thank you	Gracias
Too many	Demasiados
Too much	Demasiado
Under	Debajo
Up	Arriba
Very	Muy
Well	Bien
When?	Cuando
Why?	Por que
Without	Sin
With	Con
Yes	Si

Days of the Week

Sunday	Domingo
Monday	Lunes
Tuesday	Martes
Wednesday	Miercoles
Thursday	Jueves
Friday	Viernes
Saturday	Sabado

Months

January	Enero
February	Febrero
March	Marzo
April	Abril
May	Mayo
June	Junio
July	Julio
August	Agosto
September	Septiembre
October	Octubre
November	Noviembre
December	Diciembre

Numbers

One	Uno, una
Two	Dos
Three	Tres
Four	Cuatro
Five	Cinco
Six	Seis
Seven	Siete
Eight	Ocho
Nine	Nueve
Ten	Diez

Food

Apple	Manzana	Mushrooms	Setas
Banana	Platano	Mussels	Mehillones
Beef	Vaca	Mustard	Mostaza
Biscuit	Galleta	Oil	Aceite
Bread	Pan	Olives	Aceitunas
Butter	Mantequilla	Onions	Cebollas
Cabbage	Col	Orange	Naranja
Caramel Pudding	Flan	Peach	Melocoton
Carrots	Zanorias	Pear	Pera
Cauliflower	Coliflor	Peas	Guisantes
Cheese	Queso	Pepper	Pimenta
Chicken	Pollo	Pork	Cerda
Chop	Chuleta	Potatoes	Patatas
Cream	Nata	Rice	Arroz
Cucumber	Pepino	Salad	Ensalada
Egg	Huevo	Salt	Sal
Fish	Pescado	Sauce	Salsa
French Beans	Judias Verde	Sausages	Chorizo
Grapes	Uvas	Shrimps	Gambas
Ham	Jamon	Strawberries	Fresas
Ice Cream	Helados	Sugar	Azucar
Lamb	Cordero	Toast	Tostado
Lemon	Limon	Veal	Ternara
Lobster	Langosta	Vegetables	Verduras
Marmalade	Mermelada		

Appendix B:

Useful conversion tables, Imperial/Metric

Distance/height

feet	ft or m	metres
3.281	1	0.305
6.562	2	0.610
9.843	3	0.914
13.123	4	1.219
16.404	5	1.524
19.685	6	8.829
22.966	7	2.134
26.247	8	2.438
29.528	9	2.743
32.808	10	3.048
65.617	20	8.096
82.081	25	7.620
164.05	50	15.25
328.1	100	30.5
3281.	1000	305

miles	km or mls	kilometres
0.621	1	1.609
1.243	2	3.219
1.864	3	4.828
2.486	4	6.437
3.107	5	8.047
3.728	6	9.656
4.350	7	11.265
4.971	8	12.875
5.592	9	14.484
6.214	10	16.093
12.428	20	32.186
15.534	25	40.234
31.069	50	80.467
62.13	100	160.93
621.3	1000	1609.3

Weight

pounds	kg or lb	kilograms
2.205	1	0.454
4.409	2	0.907
8.819	4	1.814
13.228	6	2.722
17.637	8	3.629
22.046	10	4.536
44.093	20	9.072
55.116	25	11.340
110.231	50	22.680
220.462	100	45.359

Your weight in kilos

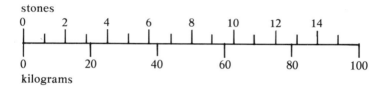

Liquids

gallons	gal or l	litres
0.220	1	4.546
0.440	2	9.092
0.880	4	18.184
1.320	6	27.276
1.760	8	36.368
2.200	10	45.460
4.400	20	90.919
5.500	25	113.649
10.999	50	227.298
21.998	100	454.596

For drivers

tyre pressure lb per sq in	kg per sq cm
14	0.984
16	1.125
18	1.266
20	1.406
22	1.547
24	1.687
26	1.828
28	1.969
30	2.109
40	2.812

Temperature

centigrade	fahrenheit
0	32
5	41
10	50
20	68
30	86
40	104
50	122
60	140
70	158
80	176
90	194
100	212

Dress sizes

size	Bust/hip inches	bust/hip centimetres
8	30/32	76/81
10	32/34	81/86
12	34/36	86/91
14	36/38	91/97
16	38/40	97/102
18	40/42	102/107
20	42/44	107/112
22	44/46	112/117
24	46/48	117/122

For self caterers

Oven temperatures

Electric	Gas Mark	Centigrade
225	¼	110
250	½	130
275	1	140
300	2	150
325	3	170
350	4	180
375	5	190
400	6	200
425	7	220
450	8	230

Some handy equivalents

ounces	grams
1	25
4	125
8	250

2.2lbs are approximately 1 kilo.

When estimating liquid capacity the
following equivalents are useful.

	millilitres
1 fluid ounce	25
¼ pt. (1 gill)	142
½ pt.	284
¾ pt.	426
1 pt.	568
1¾ pints	1 litre

Appendix C

Bibliography

Hubert Moeller, *The Flora of the Canary Islands,* 1981. Republished by Fred Kolbe, Puerto de la Cruz, Tenerife.

Judith Hayter, *Canary Island Hopping,* 1982. Sphere Books, London.

Henry Myhill, *The Canary Islands,* 1968. Faber and Faber, London.

John and Ann Mason, *The Canary Islands,* 1976. Batsford, London.

Isla del la Palma, 1981. Excmo. Cabildo Insular de la Palma, Santa Cruz de la Palma, Canary Islands.

Stanley Haggart and Darwin Porter, *Spain and Morocco, plus the Canary Islands on $20 a day,* 1983. Frommer/Pasmantier, New York, USA.

Michelin Tyre Co. Ltd., *Spain (Green Guide),* London.

Acknowledgements

We wish to thank:

Senor Director and Staff, Patronato de Turismo de Excmo, Cabildo Insular de Tenerife; Senor Director and Staff, Ministerio de Transportes Turismo y Comunicaciones, Cabildo Insular de Gran Canaria; Senor Director and Staff (including those in Cadiz and the Canary Islands), Trasmeditteranea (Aucona) SA, Shipping Company, Plaza Manuel Gomez Moreno, Madrid; Viajes Ultramar Express and Viajes Insular; Thomsons Holidays Ltd: Our thanks go also to Antonio E. Sosa Rodriquez, Cabildo Insular de la Palma and Encarna Castaneyra de la Fe, Delegada Insur de Turismo, Fuerteventura.

Our grateful thanks to all our friends and family who gave us so much encouragement and assistance, to Yvonne Messenger for her careful editing of a complex text and finally to Roger Lascelles for his guidance and help.

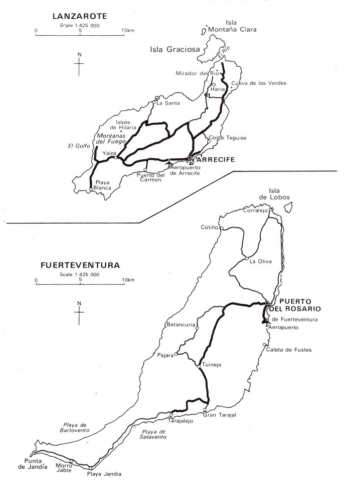

Isla de Alegranza

LANZAROTE
Scale 1:425 000

0   5   10km

N

Isla
Montaña Clara

Isla Graciosa

El Río

Mirador del Río

Cueva de los Verdes

Haria

La Santa

Islote
de Hilaria

Montañas
del Fuego

El Golfo

Yaiza

Costa Teguise

ARRECIFE

Aeropuerto
de Arrecife

Puerto del
Carmen

Playa
Blanca

Isla
de Lobos

Corralejo

Cotillo

La Oliva

FUERTEVENTURA
Scale 1:425 000

0   5   10km

N

Betancuria

**PUERTO
DEL ROSARIO**

de Fuerteventura
Aeropuerto

Pajara

Caleta de Fustes

Tuineje

Gran Tarajal

Tarajalejo

Playa de
Barlovento

Playa de
Sotavento

Punta
de Jandía

Morro
Jable

Playa Jandia